Amazing Vehicles

You Can Make

By Luc St-Amour

Fox
Chapel Publishing Co. Inc.

1970 Broad Street • East Petersburg, PA 17520 • www.carvingworld.com

Publisher: Alan Giagnocavo
Editor: Ayleen Stellhorn
Desktop Specialist: Linda L. Eberly, Eberly Designs Inc.
Cover Photography: Robert Polett

ISBN # 1–56523–150–3
Library of Congress Card Number: 00–111565

To order your copy of this book,
please send check or money order
for the cover price plus $3.00 shipping to:
Fox Books
1970 Broad Street
East Petersburg, PA 17520

Or visit us on the web at
www.carvingworld.com

Manufactured in the USA

IMPORTANT NOTICE TO PARENTS AND READERS

The models in this book are recommended only for children five years of age and up. Models contain small parts that may break and be swallowed by a young child, posing a choking hazard.

• Always use non-toxic products to finish the models.

• Use water-proof glue if the models are to be used outside.

• Check models periodically to ensure that parts have not broken or become loose.

• When using string, be sure to use pieces that are short in length to avoid injuries.

Table of Contents

Introduction

This book is for all those who enjoy building wooden models. In this edition you will find clear, easy-to-follow instructions, models that look realistic and a variety of vehicles to choose from.

We have also included details like brake lights, speedometers and treaded wheels, and suggested various types of wood to add beauty and character to your models. Two sets of full-sized patterns are provided for each model, a permanent set and a working copy which can be easily transferred onto your work in progress. Clear, concise assembly drawings are also included to guide you through the final stages. For best results, we suggest that you read all instructions before you begin.

Please keep in mind the most important aspect of woodworking - safety!

Best of luck with your projects!

How to use this book

While there are a lot of different drawings in this book, our approach is very simple. The most important thing to remember is that there are always four main steps to making our models.

In each case, read the general instructions first. They explain each step thoroughly. The first involves cutting all materials required by following the accompanying list. When all materials are cut and identified, many of the parts will already be complete. Some, however, must be finished by following the Parts Drawing section. Others can be completed by using the full-sized patterns found in the Appendix. Two sets of full-sized patterns have been provided for each model. Those in the Appendix have been printed on one-sided sheets of paper so they can be easily removed, cut out and attached to the wood. The other set, printed on both sides of the paper, should remain with the book.

Once all the parts are complete, the Assembly Drawings section for each model provides a step-by-step guide to assembling the model. Please keep the following in mind when using this book:

- Some of the models contain small parts which may break easily and pose a choking hazard for children. **(None of our models are recommended for children under the age of five!)** If you make a display model for an older child, some parts should be excluded. They have been marked with an * to the left of the List of Materials. The motorcycle is not suitable for children of any age because of it's design.

- The pick-up truck, 18 wheeler, dump truck and cement truck all use the same wheels - a total of 42 in all. While these wheels can be made using the instructions in each Parts Drawing section, they can also be purchased from most stores and mail-order catalogues to ensure consistency in size, shape and look. If you buy them, their description is as follows: outside diameter = 2", thickness = 3/4", hole = 3/8", material = hardwood. Wheels for all other models must be made in the shop. We have used a circle cutter mounted in the drill press. Make sure your material is clamped securely and turn at a very low speed.

- In the List of Materials section, please note:

  T   = Thickness
  W   = Width
  L   = Length
  Qty. = Quantity

R = Rough size. The material is cut oversized so you have ample room to apply the pattern on the surface. Sanding is not required at this point.

F = Finished size. Carefully cut and sand the part to finished size.

Recommended Tools

Because of the complexity of the models, the use of power tools is a must. They will not only give you the precision needed but will also save you an enormous amount of time.

For some parts you will be required to make intricate inside cuts. The best tool for this task is the scroll saw. A drill press must also be used to drill holes in the centre of the dowel. (A hand drill is not suitable for this task.)

For sanding purposes, you will need power sanders to save you time and give better results.

The wood needed to make these projects varies in thicknesses which are not standard. This means you will need to use a thickness planner and a bandsaw to re-saw and bring the wood to the specified thickness. (Some of you may have access to these tools at school, from friends or at a store.)

Accessories Needed

- Drill bit set (1/16" to 1/2")
- Flat drill bit set (3/8" to 1")
- Measuring tape
- Combination square
- Sanding drum set
- Wood vice
- Assorted c-clamps
- Awl (Scriber)
- Wood glue
- Wood file
- Pencil and eraser
- 12"ruler(clear recommended)
- Compass
- Circle cutter

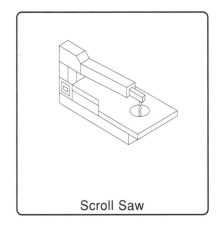
Scroll Saw

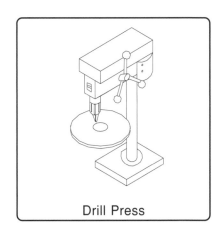
Drill Press

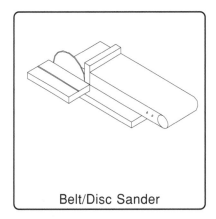
Belt/Disc Sander

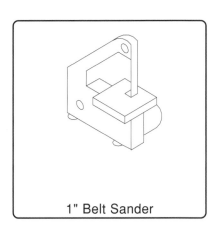
1" Belt Sander

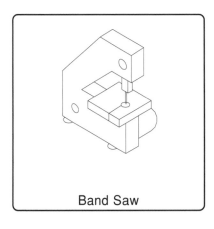
Band Saw

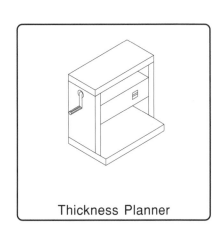
Thickness Planner

PICK-UP TRUCK

Step 1   Start by cutting materials needed using the List of Materials on page 10. **Pay attention to the rough and finished size, and identify parts as they are cut.**

Please note: Different types of wood can be used for the various parts. It is suggested, however, that hard wood be used since many of the parts would be much too fragile if using soft wood. We have used a combination of Maple, Pine, Oak and exotic woods such as Padauk (dark wood), Yellowheart (light colour) and Mahogany (dark wood) to give the models a nice contrast!

Step 2   Parts P1 to P8 are already complete. Parts P9 to P13 will need a few more steps. See the Parts Drawing section on page 11 for more details.

Step 3   Parts P14 to P20 require removing the Full-Sized Patterns sheet found on page 95 of the Appendix. Cut out the patterns, leaving approximately 1/16" all around, and place on the proper piece of wood. Patterns can be secured to the wood using either spray adhesive or rubber cement. If using the latter, cut and sand the part first to finished size. If drilling is required, mark the hole by inserting an awl or nail through the pattern into the wood. Remove the pattern before drilling.

Step 4   Follow the assembly drawings on pages 13 and 14 to complete your model.

Please note: In order for this model to move properly, it is recommended that you apply a lubricant to wheel shafts and axle block holes. Lard is the cheapest and safest option. It is non-toxic and found in most households.

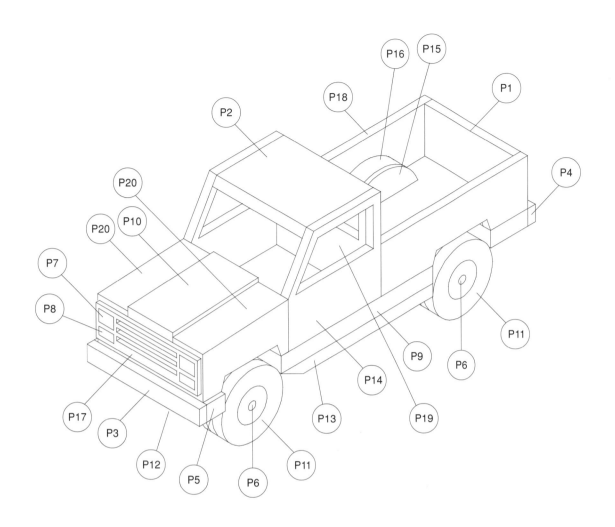

Optional Accessories

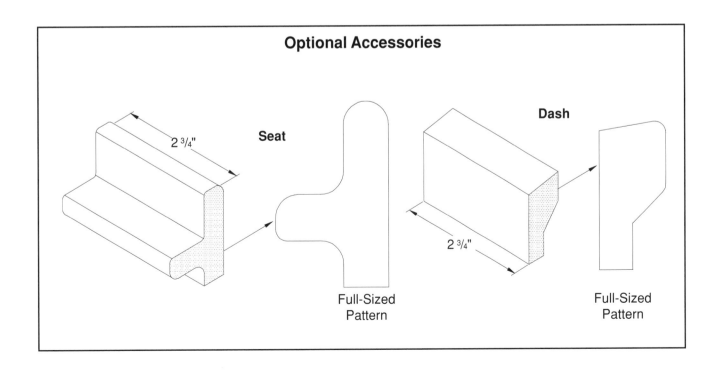

Seat

2 ³/₄"

Full-Sized Pattern

Dash

2 ³/₄"

Full-Sized Pattern

Part	Description	Qty.	T	W	L	Material	*
P1	End Pieces	2	1/4"	1 1/2"	3"	Oak	F
P2	Roof	1	1/4"	2 1/2"	3"	Oak	F
P3	Front Bumper	1	1/4"	1/2"	3 3/4"	Dark Wood	F
P4	Rear Bumper	1	1/4"	1/2"	3 1/2"	Dark Wood	F
P5	Bumper Sides	2	1/4"	1/2"	5/8"	Dark Wood	F
P6	Wheel Shafts	2	3/8" dia.		3 1/2"	Maple Dowel	F
* P7	Main Headlights	2	1/8"	3/8"	1/2"	Light Colour	F
* P8	Flashers	2	1/8"	1/4"	1/2"	Dark Wood	F
P9	Main Frame	1	1/2"	3 1/2"	11"	Oak	F
P10	Hood Centre	1	1 1/2"	1 5/8"	2 7/8"	Oak	F
P11	Wheels	4	3/4"	2" dia.		Maple	F
P12	Axle Blocks	2	3/4"	3/4"	2 1/4"	Maple	F
P13	Floor Boards	2	1/8"	3/4"	5 1/8"	Dark Wood	F
P14	Cabin Sides	2	1/4"	3 1/4"	3 1/4"	Oak	R
P15	Wheel Covers	2	1/8"	1"	2 5/8"	Oak	R
P16	Wheel Covers	2	1/2"	1"	2 5/8"	Oak	R
P17	Grill	1	1/8"	1 1/4"	3 5/8"	Dark Wood	R
P18	Box Sides	2	1/4"	1 3/4"	5 1/4"	Oak	R
P19	Cabin Back	1	1/4"	3 1/4"	3"	Oak	R
P20	Hood Sides	2	1"	1 3/4"	3 1/8"	Oak	R

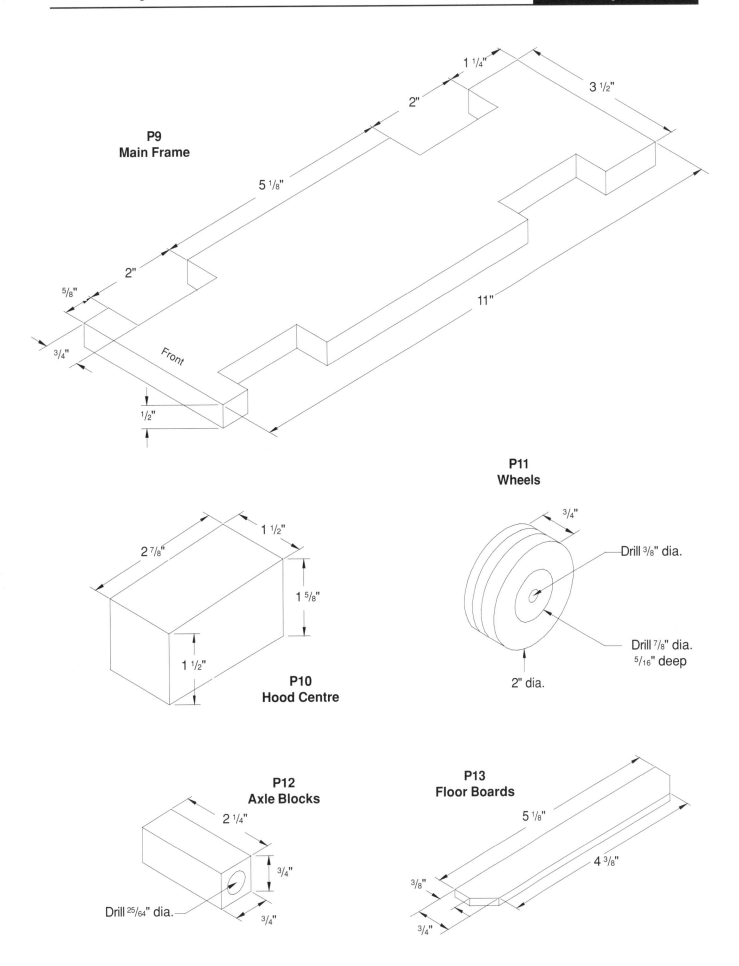

P9
Main Frame

1 1/4"

2"

3 1/2"

5 1/8"

2"

5/8"

3/4"

Front

11"

1/2"

P11
Wheels

3/4"

Drill 3/8" dia.

Drill 7/8" dia.
5/16" deep

2" dia.

1 1/2"

2 7/8"

1 5/8"

1 1/2"

P10
Hood Centre

P12
Axle Blocks

2 1/4"

3/4"

Drill 25/64" dia.

3/4"

P13
Floor Boards

5 1/8"

4 3/8"

3/8"

3/4"

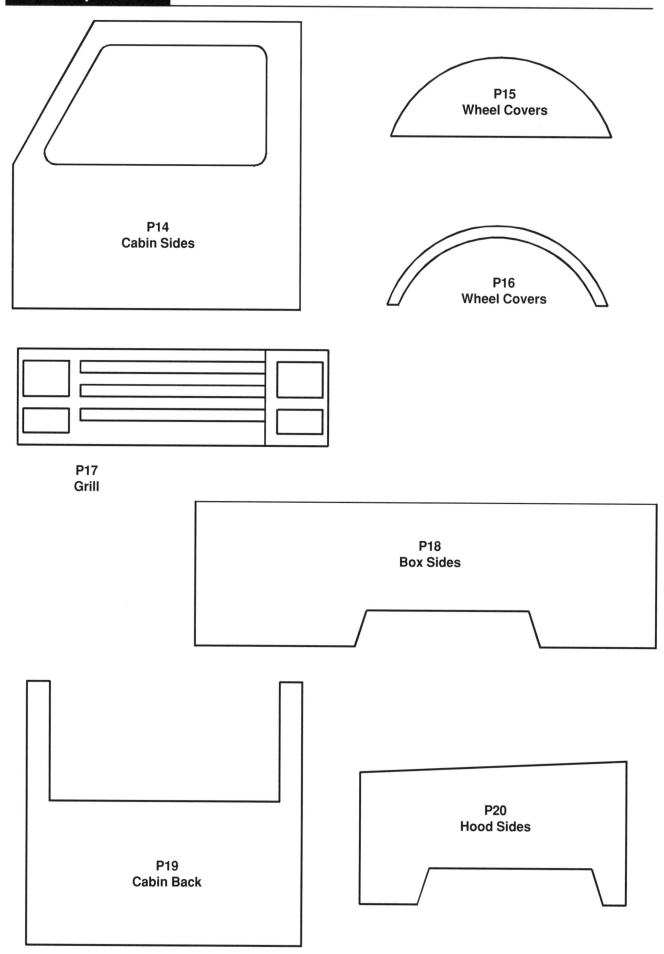

P15
Wheel Covers

P16
Wheel Covers

P14
Cabin Sides

P17
Grill

P18
Box Sides

P19
Cabin Back

P20
Hood Sides

1

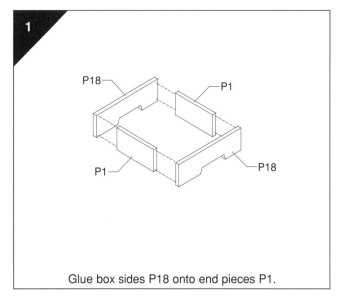

Glue box sides P18 onto end pieces P1.

2

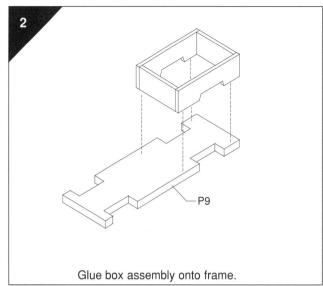

Glue box assembly onto frame.

3

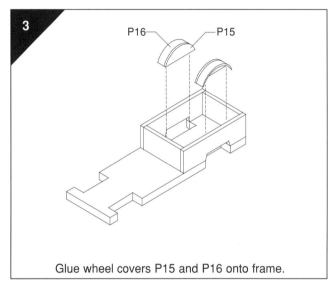

Glue wheel covers P15 and P16 onto frame.

4

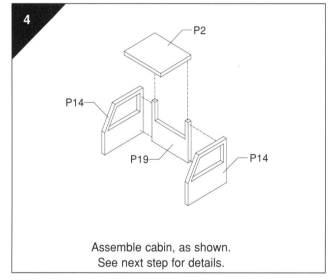

Assemble cabin, as shown.
See next step for details.

5

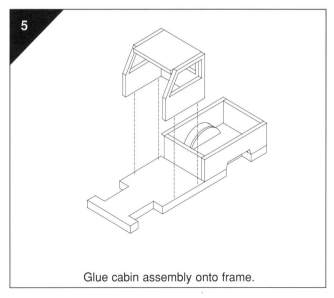

Glue cabin assembly onto frame.

6

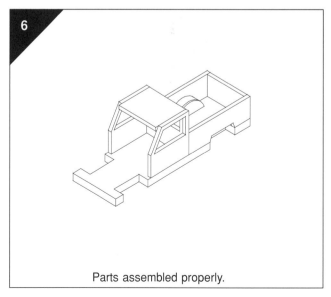

Parts assembled properly.

7

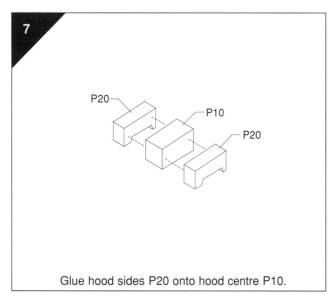

Glue hood sides P20 onto hood centre P10.

8

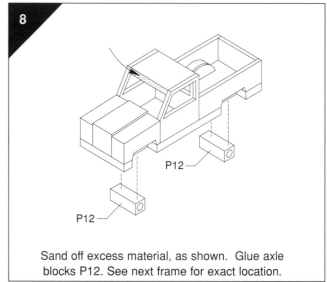

Sand off excess material, as shown. Glue axle blocks P12. See next frame for exact location.

9

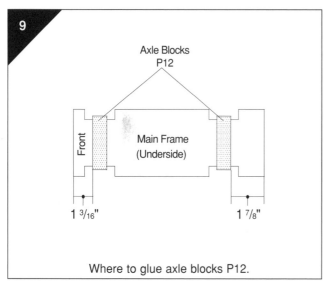

Where to glue axle blocks P12.

10

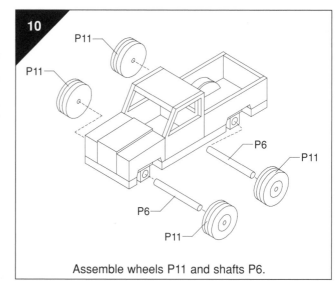

Assemble wheels P11 and shafts P6.

11

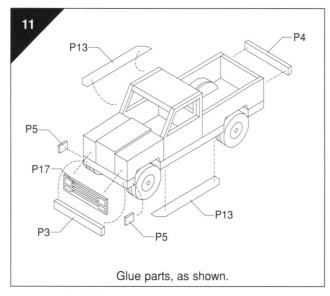

Glue parts, as shown.

12

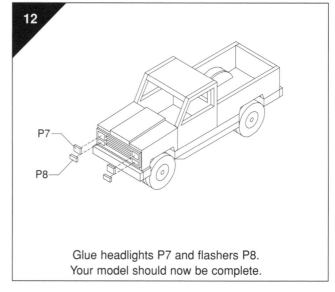

Glue headlights P7 and flashers P8.
Your model should now be complete.

RACING CAR

Step 1

Start by cutting materials needed using the List of Materials on page 17. **Pay attention to the rough and finished size, and identify parts as they are cut.**

Please note: Different types of wood can be used for the various parts. It is suggested, however, that hard wood be used since many of the parts would be much too fragile if using soft wood. We have used a combination of Maple, Pine, Oak and exotic woods such as Padauk (dark wood), Yellowheart (light colour) and Mahogany (dark wood) to give the models a nice contrast!

Step 2

Parts C1 to C3 are already complete. Parts C4 to C6 will need a few more steps. See the Parts Drawing section on page 18 for more details.

Step 3

Parts C7 to C13 require removing the Full-Sized Patterns sheet found on pages 97 and 99 of the Appendix. Cut out the patterns, leaving approximately 1/16" all around, and place on the proper piece of wood. Patterns can be secured to the wood using either spray adhesive or rubber cement. If using the latter, cut and sand the part first to finished size. If drilling is required, mark the hole by inserting an awl or nail through the pattern into the wood. Remove the pattern before drilling.

Step 4

Follow the assembly drawings on pages 21 and 22 to complete your model.

Please note: In order for this model to move properly, it is recommended that you apply a lubricant to wheels shafts. Lard is the cheapest and safest option. It is non-toxic and found in most households.

Using a rasp and/or sand paper, round all edges of the main body, wheels and upper vent to make these parts aerodynamic and realistic.

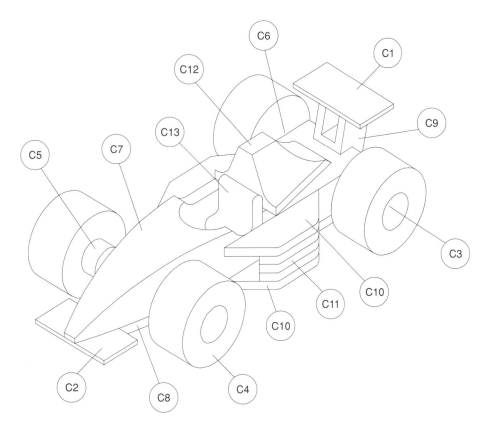

Part	Description	Qty.	T	W	L	Material	*
C1	Rear Spoiler	1	1/8"	1 1/4"	2 1/2"	Dark Wood	F
C2	Front Spoiler	1	1/8"	1 1/4"	2 1/2"	Dark Wood	F
C3	Wheel Shafts	2	1/4" dia.		4"	Maple Dowel	F
C4	Wheels	4	1 1/4"	2" dia.		Dark Wood	F
C5	Front Wheel Spacers	2	1/2"	3/4" dia.		Maple	F
C6	Rear Wheel Spacers	2	1/4"	3/4" dia.		Maple	F
C7	Main Body	1	1 1/2"	2 1/2"	10 1/4"	Pine	R
C8	Main Frame	1	1/4"	2 1/2"	9"	Maple	R
C9	Spoiler Support	1	1"	1 1/8"	2 3/4"	Maple	R
C10	Side Vent Covers	4	1/4"	1 1/4"	3 3/4"	Pine	R
C11	Side Vent Sides	6	1/4"	1 1/4"	3 1/4"	4 dark, 2 light	R
C12	Upper Vent	1	1 3/4"	2 5/8"	2 7/8"	Pine	R
C13	Seat	1	1 1/4"	1 1/2"	1 7/8"	Dark Wood	R

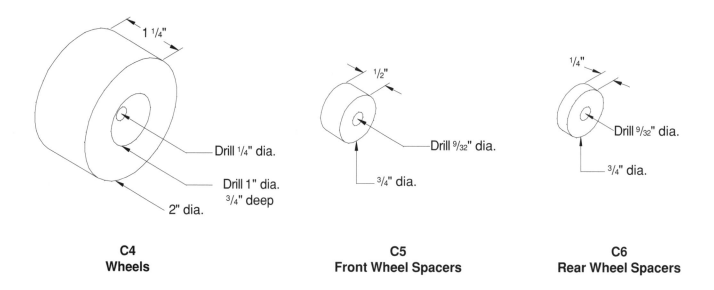

1 1/4"

Drill 1/4" dia.

Drill 1" dia.
3/4" deep

2" dia.

C4
Wheels

1/2"

Drill 9/32" dia.

3/4" dia.

C5
Front Wheel Spacers

1/4"

Drill 9/32" dia.

3/4" dia.

C6
Rear Wheel Spacers

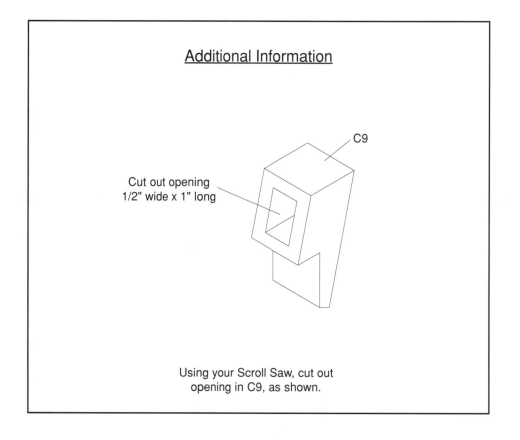

Additional Information

C9

Cut out opening
1/2" wide x 1" long

Using your Scroll Saw, cut out
opening in C9, as shown.

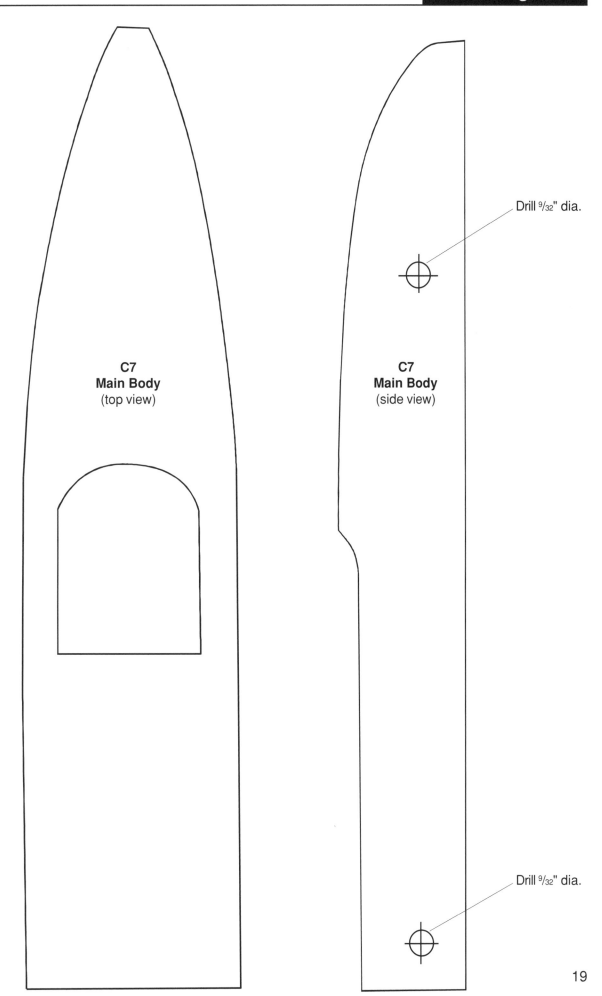

C7
Main Body
(top view)

C7
Main Body
(side view)

Drill ⁹/₃₂" dia.

Drill ⁹/₃₂" dia.

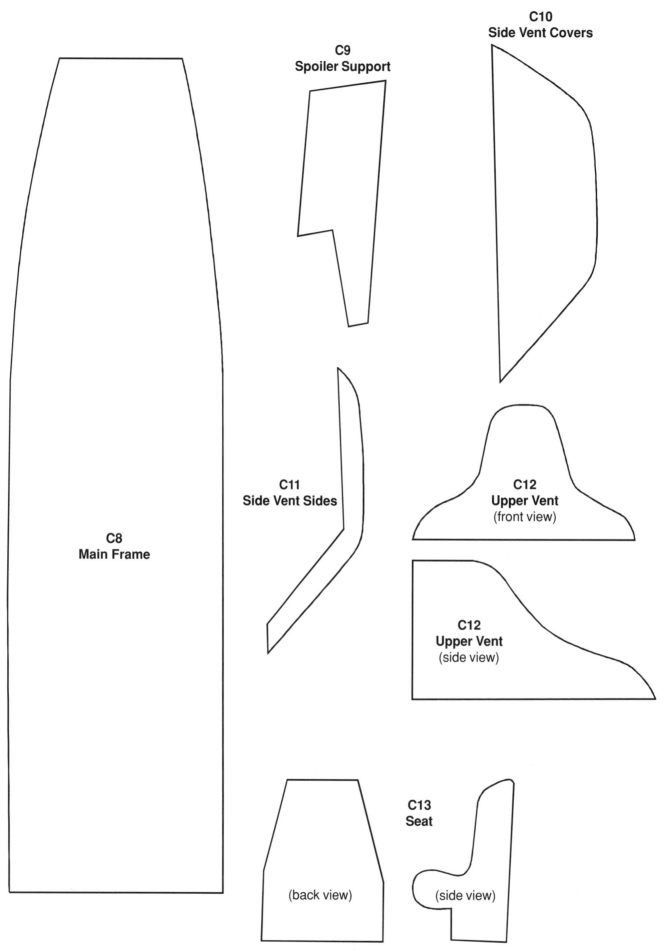

C9
Spoiler Support

C10
Side Vent Covers

C11
Side Vent Sides

C8
Main Frame

C12
Upper Vent
(front view)

C12
Upper Vent
(side view)

C13
Seat

(back view)

(side view)

1

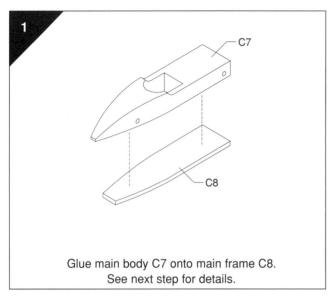

Glue main body C7 onto main frame C8.
See next step for details.

2

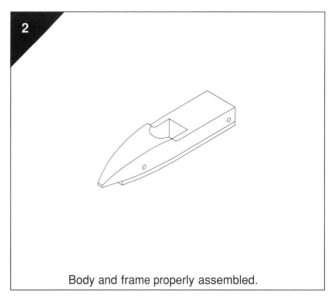

Body and frame properly assembled.

3

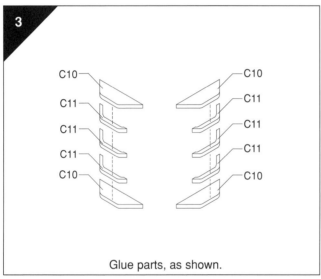

Glue parts, as shown.

4

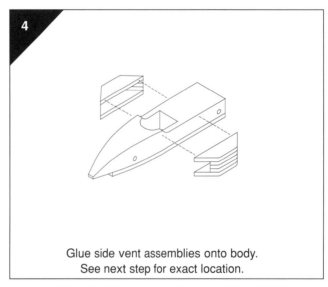

Glue side vent assemblies onto body.
See next step for exact location.

5

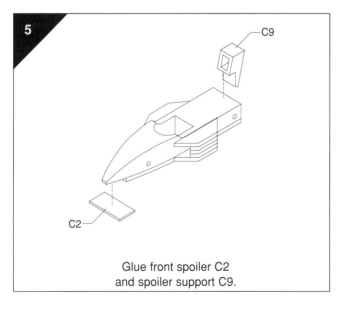

Glue front spoiler C2
and spoiler support C9.

6

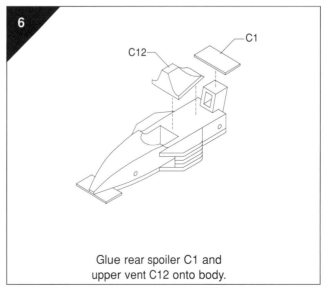

Glue rear spoiler C1 and
upper vent C12 onto body.

12

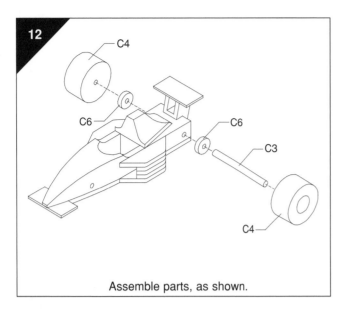

Assemble parts, as shown.

12

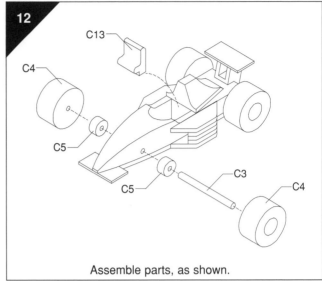

Assemble parts, as shown.

12

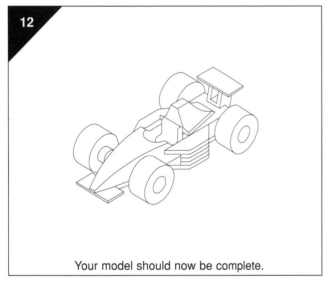

Your model should now be complete.

MOTORCYCLE

Step 1

Start by cutting materials needed using the List of Materials on page 25. **Pay attention to the rough and finished size, and identify parts as they are cut.**

Please note: Different types of wood can be used for the various parts. It is suggested, however, that hard wood be used since many of the parts would be much too fragile if using soft wood. We have used a combination of Maple, Pine, Oak and exotic woods such as Padauk (dark wood), Yellowheart (light colour) and Mahogany (dark wood) to give the models a nice contrast!

Step 2

Parts M1 to M6 are already complete. Parts M7 to M9 will need a few more steps. See the Parts Drawing section on page 26 for more details.

Step 3.

Parts M11 to M30 require removing the Full-Sized Patterns sheet found on pages 101 and 103 of the Appendix. Cut out the patterns, leaving approximately 1/16" all around, and place on the proper piece of wood. Patterns can be secured to the wood using either spray adhesive or rubber cement. If using the latter, cut and sand the part first to finished size. If drilling is required, mark the hole by inserting an awl or nail through the pattern into the wood. Remove the pattern before drilling.

To make the wheels, see instructions on pages 26 and 27.

Step 4

Follow the assembly drawings on pages 30 to 32 to complete your model.

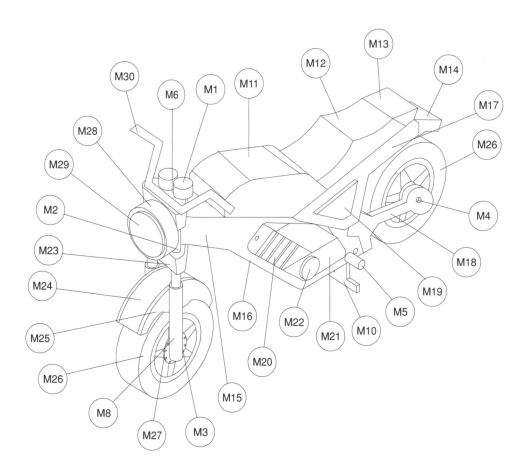

Part	Description	Qty.	T	W	L	Material	*
M1	Speedometer & Tachometer	2	$1/2$" dia.		$3/8$"	Maple Dowel	F
M2	Upper Front Forks	2	$1/4$" dia.		$2\,3/4$"	Maple Dowel	F
M3	Front Wheel Shaft	1	$1/4$" dia.		$1\,1/2$"	Maple Dowel	F
M4	Rear Wheel Shaft	1	$1/4$" dia.		$1\,1/2$"	Maple Dowel	F
M5	Foot Pegs	2	$1/4$" dia.		$3/8$"	Maple Dowel	F
M6	Steering Shaft	1	$1/4$" dia.		$1\,1/2$"	Maple Dowel	F
M7	Rear Shocks	2	$3/8$" dia.		3"	Maple Dowel	R
M8	Lower Front Forks	2	$3/8$" dia.		$2\,1/8$"	Maple Dowel	F
M9	Muffler	1	$1/2$" dia.		$3\,3/4$"	Maple Dowel	R
M10	Kick Stand	1	see drawing page 29			Maple	
M11	Fuel Tank	1	$1\,1/2$"	$1\,7/8$"	$2\,7/8$"	Dark Wood	R
M12	Seat	1	$3/4$"	$1\,5/8$"	$3\,1/8$"	Dark Wood	R
M13	Seat Brace	1	$1/2$"	$1\,1/4$"	$3/4$"	Dark Wood	R
M14	Rear Fender	1	$3/4$"	$1\,1/4$"	$1\,1/2$"	Dark Wood	R
M15	Frame - Part 1 of 4	1	1"	2"	1"	Oak	R
M16	Frame - Part 2 & 3 of 4	2	$1/4$"	$3\,1/4$"	$3\,1/2$"	Oak	R
M17	Frame - Part 4 of 4	1	$1\,3/4$"	$1\,7/8$"	4"	Oak	R
M18	Swing Arm	1	$1\,1/2$"	$1\,3/4$"	$2\,3/4$"	Oak	R
M19	Side Covers	2	$1/8$"	$1\,1/8$"	$2\,1/8$"	Dark Wood	R
M20	Engine Top	1	$1\,1/2$"	$1\,3/4$"	$1\,3/8$"	Pine	R

Part	Description	Qty.	T	W	L	Material	*
M21	Engine Base	1	1"	2"	2"	Maple	R
M22	Engine Covers	2	1/8"	3/4" dia.		Dark Wood	F
M23	Fork Frames	2	1/4"	2 1/8"	1 1/4"	Maple	R
M24	Fender - Centre Piece	1	7/8"	1 1/2"	2 3/4"	Dark Wood	R
M25	Fender Sides	2	1/16"	1 1/2"	2 3/4"	Dark Wood	R
M26	Wheels	2	3/4"	3 1/4" dia.		Maple	F
M27	Disk Brakes	3	1/8"	1 1/4"	1 1/4"	Maple	R
M28	Headlight Frame	1	5/8"	1 1/2"	1 1/2"	Maple	R
M29	Headlight	1	1/8"	1 1/8" dia.		Light Colour	F
M30	Handlebars	1	1/4"	1 7/8"	4"	Maple	R

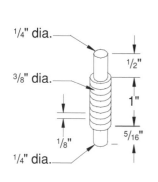

M7
Rear Shocks

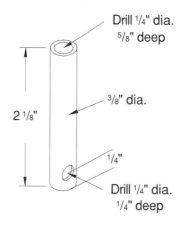

M8
Lower Front Forks

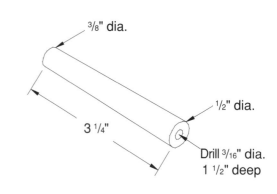

M9
Muffler

Recommended Jig
for wheel construction

Material required for this jig

- 1/4" x 1 3/4" bolt
- 1/4" dia. washer
- 1/4" nut

Take the bolt and remove the head. Mount the bolt to the drill chuck. Slide wheel onto bolt. Secure with washer and nut.

Steps for making the wheels

Important: Always unplug your drill press before making any adjustments, keep hands away from revolving cutter and clamp material securely before making any cuts.

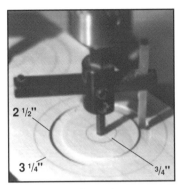

Step 1: From 3/4" maple, cut a piece 4" wide by 12" long. Use a compass to trace the three diameters for each wheel, marking the centre. Install circle cutter in drill press chuck and line up pilot bit with the centre mark for the first wheel. Clamp material securely and set drill press at a very low speed. Take a first cut 1/16" deep, while staying inside the 2 1/2" diameter circle. Adjust the cutter inward and take a second cut, again 1/16" deep.

Step 1

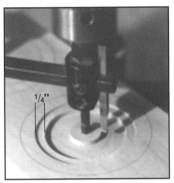

Step 2: Trace a guideline 1/4" inside the 2 1/2" diameter. Adjust your cutter to this new guide and take a series of cuts (1/16" deeper than the first step) going towards the centre. Stop when you reach the 3/4" diameter circle. Unclamp the material and repeat the first two steps on the opposite side. Follow the same procedures for the second wheel.

Step 2

Step 3: Cut out the two patterns marked M26 on page 103. Use them to transfer the guidelines onto your wheel.

Step 3

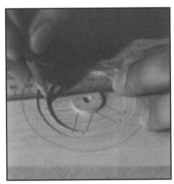

Step 4: Remove pattern and draw a straight line from outer guideline marks to inner marks.

Step 4

Step 5: Use your scroll saw to remove area between spokes.

Step 5

Step 6: Cut wheel from stock using outer diameter as a guideline. Sand outer wheel until well rounded.

Step 6

Step 7: Re-drill centre hole, this time using a 1/4" bit. Mount wheel as described on previous page. Using a low speed, file the outer edges to round off corners.

Step 7

Step 8: Use a triangular file to make narrow grooves on wheel surface. Grooves should be approximately 1/8" apart. Re-drill centre hole, this time using a 9/32" bit. Your wheel should now be complete.

Step 8

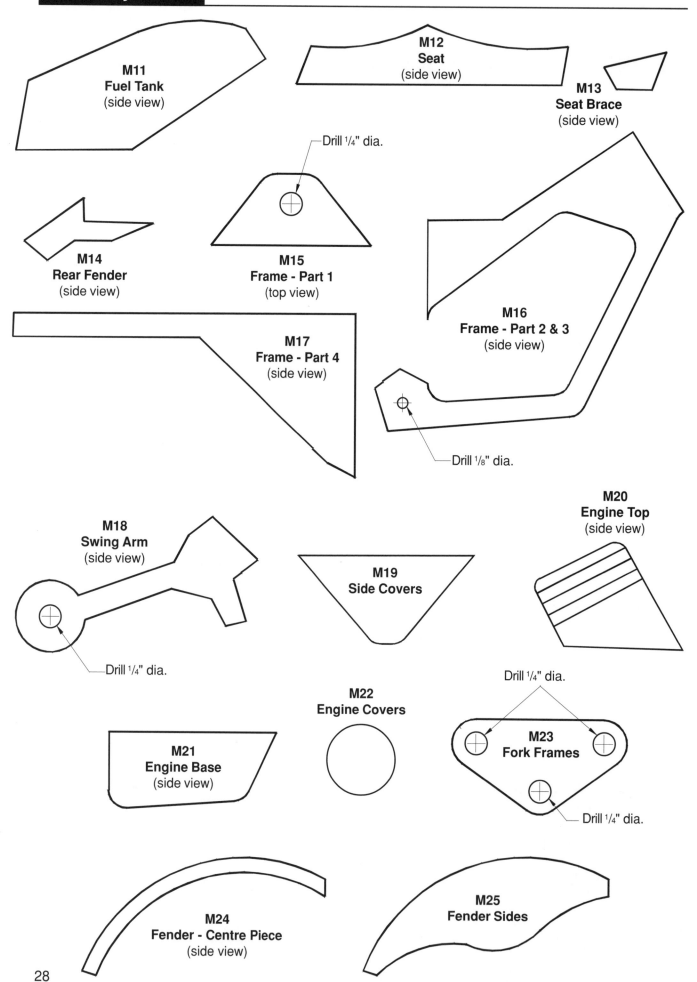

M11
Fuel Tank
(side view)

M12
Seat
(side view)

M13
Seat Brace
(side view)

Drill ¼" dia.

M14
Rear Fender
(side view)

M15
Frame - Part 1
(top view)

M16
Frame - Part 2 & 3
(side view)

M17
Frame - Part 4
(side view)

Drill ⅛" dia.

M18
Swing Arm
(side view)

M19
Side Covers

M20
Engine Top
(side view)

Drill ¼" dia.

M21
Engine Base
(side view)

M22
Engine Covers

M23
Fork Frames

Drill ¼" dia.

Drill ¼" dia.

M24
Fender - Centre Piece
(side view)

M25
Fender Sides

Full-Sized Patterns: Set One

Motorcycle

M26
Wheels
(see details page 27)

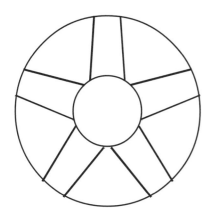

M27
Disk Brakes

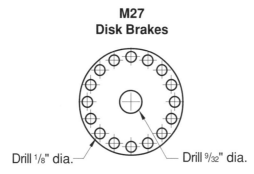

Drill ⅛" dia.

Drill ⁹⁄₃₂" dia.

M28
Headlight Frame

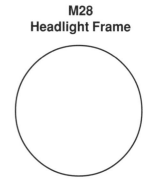

M29
Headlight

M30
Handlebars

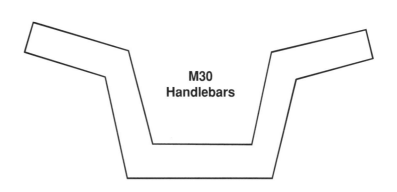

Additional Information

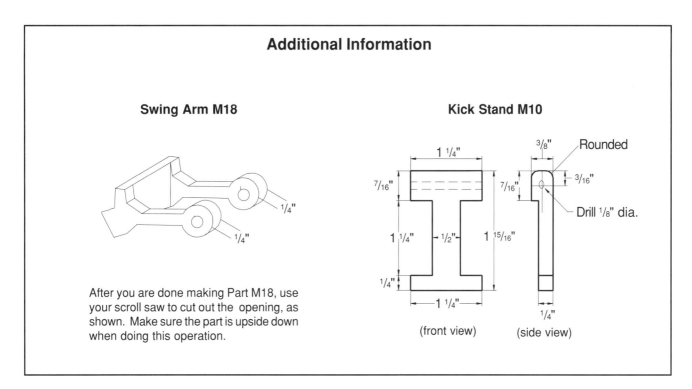

Swing Arm M18

¼"

¼"

After you are done making Part M18, use your scroll saw to cut out the opening, as shown. Make sure the part is upside down when doing this operation.

Kick Stand M10

1 ¼"

7/16"

1 ¼"   ½"

¼"

1 ¼"

(front view)

3/8"   Rounded

7/16"

3/16"

Drill ⅛" dia.

1 ¹⁵⁄₁₆"

¼"

(side view)

1

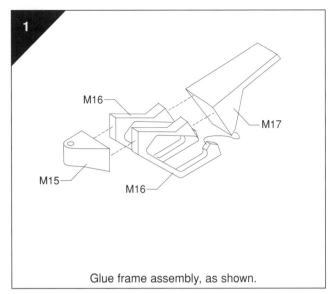

M16

M17

M15

M16

Glue frame assembly, as shown.

2

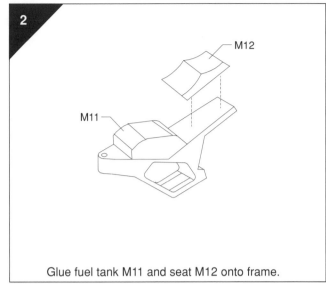

M12

M11

Glue fuel tank M11 and seat M12 onto frame.

3

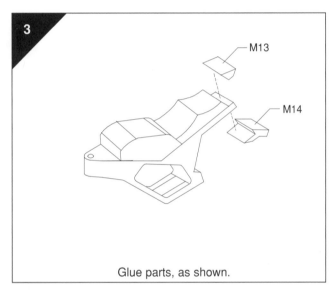

M13

M14

Glue parts, as shown.

4

Top view

1 3/8"

Sand each side to remove sections shown in grey.

1"

Holding this assembly upright, sand each sides, as shown .

5

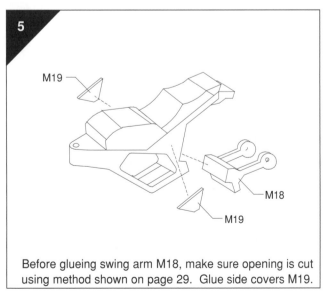

M19

M18

M19

Before glueing swing arm M18, make sure opening is cut using method shown on page 29. Glue side covers M19.

6

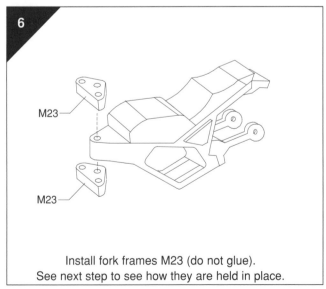

M23

M23

Install fork frames M23 (do not glue). See next step to see how they are held in place.

7

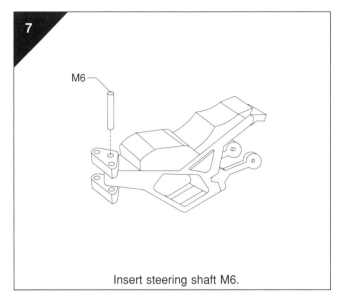

Insert steering shaft M6.

8

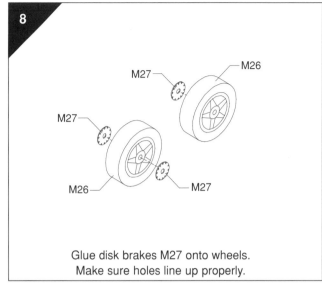

Glue disk brakes M27 onto wheels.
Make sure holes line up properly.

9

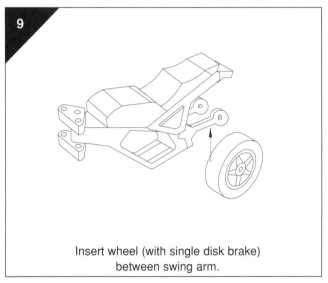

Insert wheel (with single disk brake)
between swing arm.

10

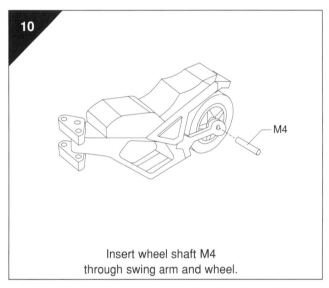

Insert wheel shaft M4
through swing arm and wheel.

11

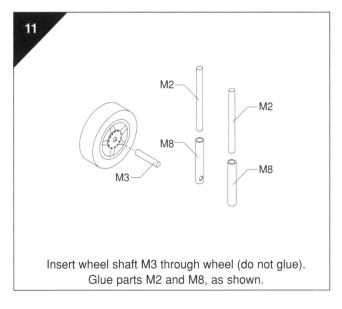

Insert wheel shaft M3 through wheel (do not glue).
Glue parts M2 and M8, as shown.

12

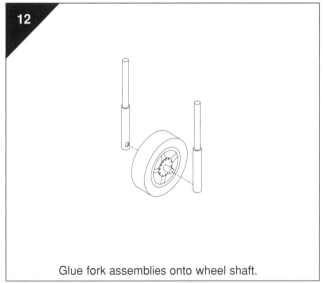

Glue fork assemblies onto wheel shaft.

13

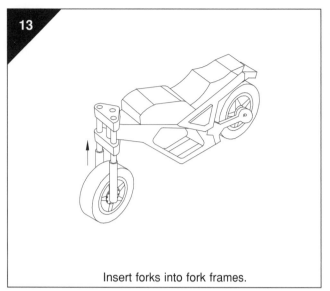

Insert forks into fork frames.

14

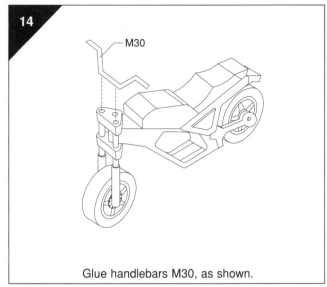

M30

Glue handlebars M30, as shown.

15

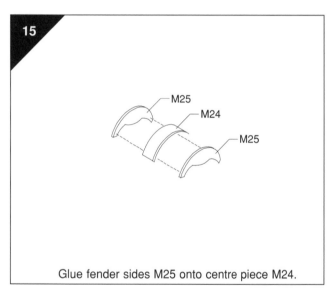

M25

M24

M25

Glue fender sides M25 onto centre piece M24.

16

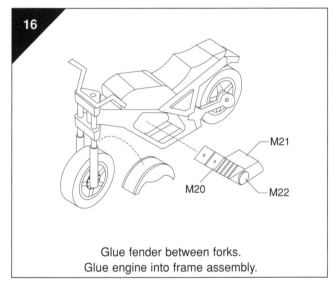

M21

M20

M22

Glue fender between forks.
Glue engine into frame assembly.

17

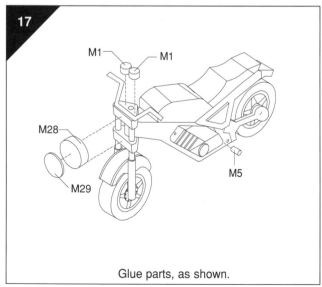

M1   M1

M28

M29

M5

Glue parts, as shown.

18

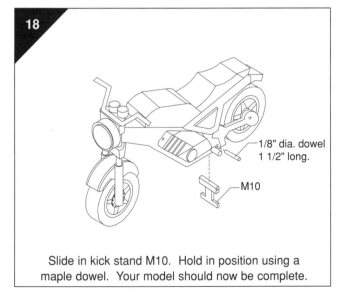

1/8" dia. dowel
1 1/2" long.

M10

Slide in kick stand M10. Hold in position using a
maple dowel. Your model should now be complete.

AIRLINER

Step 1   Start by cutting materials needed using the List of Materials on page 35. **Pay attention to the rough and finished size, and identify parts as they are cut.**

Please note: Different types of wood can be used for the various parts. It is suggested, however, that hard wood be used since many of the parts would be much too fragile if using soft wood. We have used a combination of Maple, Pine, Oak and exotic woods such as Padauk (dark wood), Yellowheart (light colour) and Mahogany (dark wood) to give the models a nice contrast!

Step 2   Parts A2 and A4 are already complete. Parts A1 and A3 will need a few more steps. See the Parts Drawing section on page 36 for more details.

Step 3   Parts A5 to A9 require removing the Full-Sized Patterns sheet found on pages 103 and 105 of the Appendix. Cut out the patterns, leaving approximately 1/16" all around, and place on the proper piece of wood. Patterns can be secured to the wood using either spray adhesive or rubber cement. If using the latter, cut and sand the part first to finished size. If drilling is required, mark the hole by inserting an awl or nail through the pattern into the wood. Remove the pattern before drilling.

Step 4   The Detailed Drawing on page 35 shows where to glue each part.

Additional Information: Using a rasp and/or sand paper, shape all parts to make them realistic and aerodynamic.

Once the engine frames (parts A9) are cut and sanded to finished size, additional sanding is required to ensure that they fit the contour of the wings.

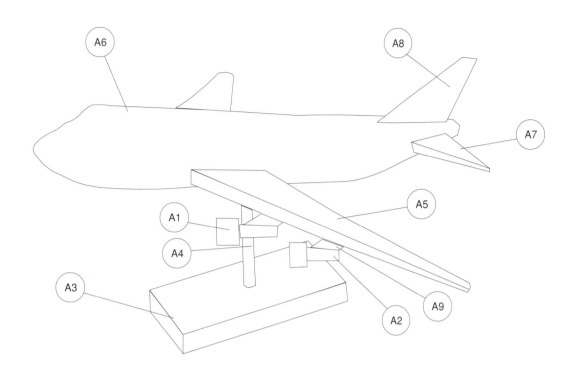

	Part	Description	Qty.	**T**	**W**	**L**	Material	*
*	A1	Engines	4	½" dia.		⅜"	Maple Dowel	F
*	A2	Engine Supports	4	¼" dia.		⅞"	Maple Dowel	F
	A3	Base	1	¾"	1 ¾"	4 ¼"	Oak	F
	A4	Base Dowel	1	¼" dia.		3 ½"	Maple Dowel	F
	A5	Wings	2	⅜"	2 ⅛"	6 ¾"	Pine	R
	A6	Fuselage	1	1 ½"	1 ¾"	11 ¼"	Pine	R
	A7	Stabilizers	2	¼"	1 ¾"	2"	Pine	R
	A8	Vertical Fin	1	¼"	1 ⅞"	3"	Pine	R
*	A9	Engine Frames	4	⅛"	½"	1 ¾"	Maple	R

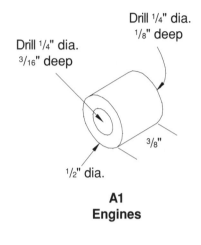

Drill ¼" dia.
³⁄₁₆" deep

Drill ¼" dia.
⅛" deep

½" dia.

³⁄₈"

A1
Engines

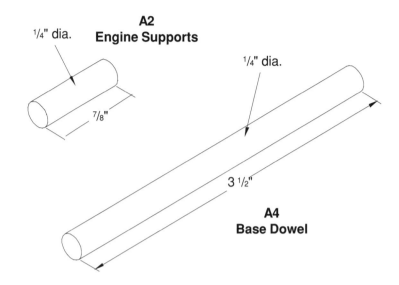

A2
Engine Supports

¼" dia.

⅞"

¼" dia.

3 ½"

A4
Base Dowel

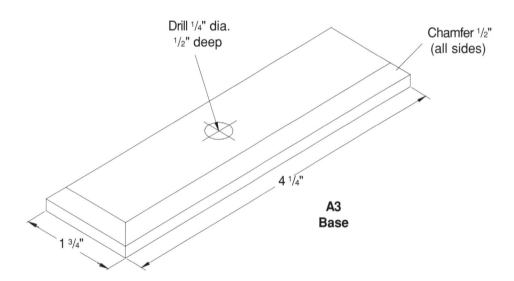

Drill ¼" dia.
½" deep

Chamfer ½"
(all sides)

4 ¼"

1 ³⁄₄"

A3
Base

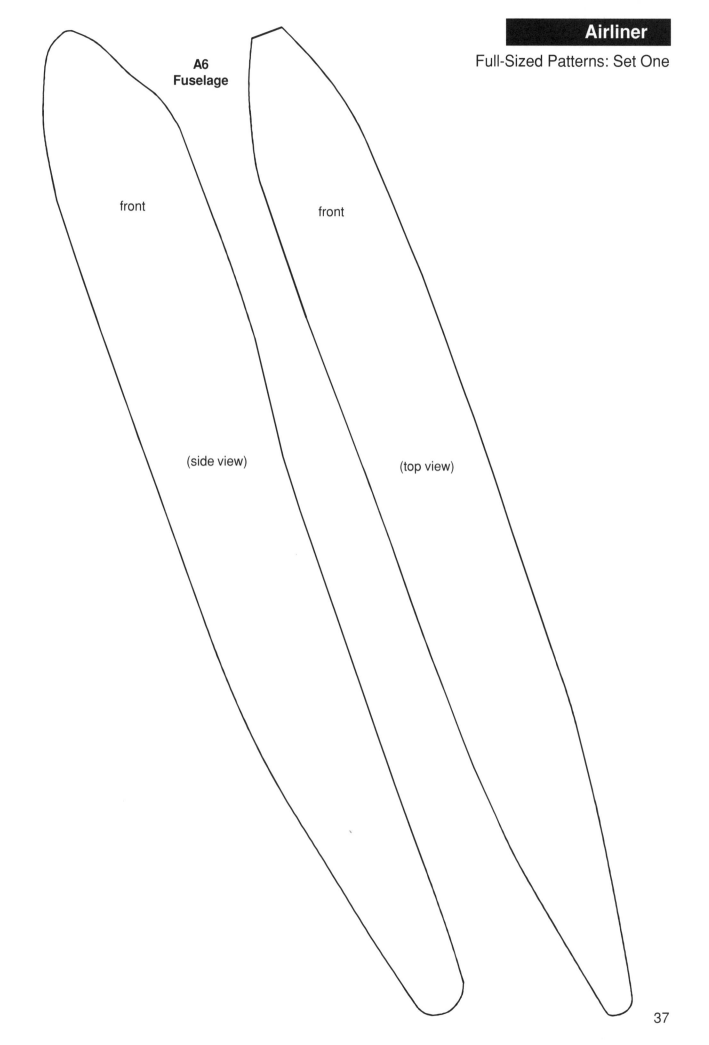

**A6
Fuselage**

front

(side view)

front

(top view)

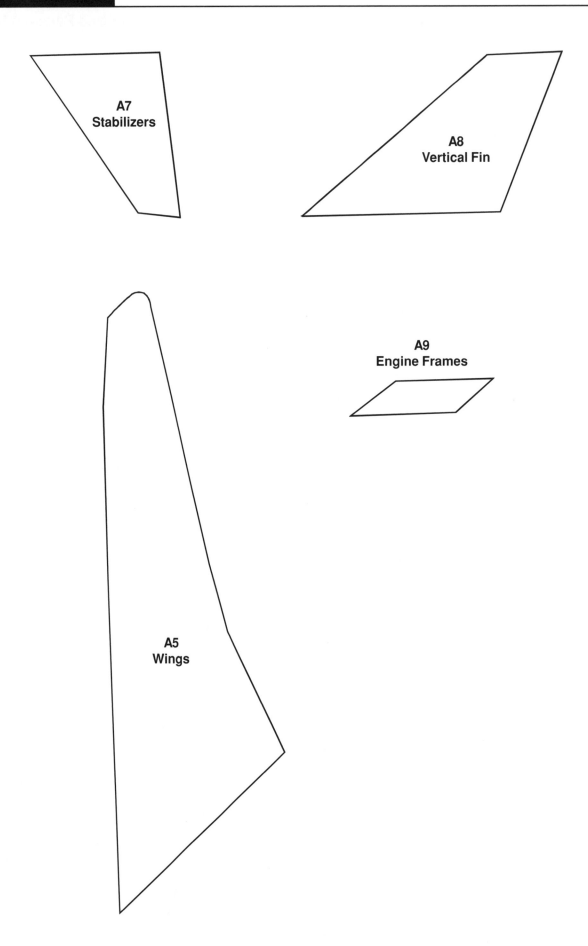

A7
Stabilizers

A8
Vertical Fin

A9
Engine Frames

A5
Wings

TRAIN SET

Step 1

Start by cutting materials needed using the List of Materials on page 10. **Pay attention to the rough and finished size, and identify parts as they are cut.**

Please note: Different types of wood can be used for the various parts. It is suggested, however, that hard wood be used since many of the parts would be much too fragile if using soft wood. We have used a combination of Maple, Pine, Oak and exotic woods such as Padauk (dark wood), Yellowheart (light colour) and Mahogany (dark wood) to give the models a nice contrast!

Step 2

Engine: Parts T1 to T10 are already complete. Parts T11 to T15, T24 and T25 will need a few more steps. See the Parts Drawing section on page 43 for more details.

Coal Car: Parts TC1 to TC5 are already complete. Part TC6 will need a few more steps. See the Parts Drawing section on page 49 for more details.

Passenger Car: Parts TP1 to TP5 are already complete. Parts TP6 to TP9 will need a few more steps. See the Parts Drawing section on page 52 for more details.

Caboose: Parts TL1 and TL2 are already complete. Parts TL3 to TL5 will need a few more steps. See the Parts Drawing section on page 57 for more details.

Step 3

Engine: Parts T16 to T28 require removing the Full-Sized Patterns sheet found on pages 107 and 109 of the Appendix.

Coal Car: Parts TC7 to TC10 require removing the Full-Sized Patterns sheet found on page 109 of the Appendix.

Passenger Car: Parts TP10 to TP14 require removing the Full-Sized Patterns sheet found on page 111 of the Appendix.

Caboose: Parts TL6 to TL12 require removing the Full-Sized Patterns sheet found on page 113 of the Appendix.

Cut out the patterns, leaving approximately 1/16" all around, and place on the proper piece of wood. Patterns can be secured to the wood using either spray adhesive or rubber cement. If using the latter, cut and sand the part first to finished size. If drilling is required, mark the hole by inserting an awl or nail through the pattern into the wood. Remove the pattern before drilling.

Step 4

Follow the assembly drawings to complete your model. (Engine: page 45 to 47; Coal Car: page 50; Passenger Car: pages 54 and 55; Caboose: pages 59 and 60.)

Please note: If you wish to display your train set, you can make a track using the drawing found on page 57.

Important: In order for this model to move properly, it is recommended that you apply a lubricant to wheel shafts and axle block holes. Lard is the cheapest and safest option. It is non-toxic and found in most households.

	Part	Description	Qty.	T	W	L	Material	*
	T1	Cabin Front	1	1/4"	2 1/4"	2 1/2"	Oak	F
	T2	Boiler Base - 1	1	1/4"	1 1/4"	6 3/8"	Light Colour	F
	T3	Boiler Base - 2	1	1/4"	1 1/4"	6 3/8"	Dark Wood	F
*	T4	Runners	2	1/8"	3/8"	6 3/8"	Dark Wood	F
	T5	Main Boiler Vent	1	1/2" dia.		3/4"	Dark Dowel	F
	T6	Secondary Boiler Vents	2	1/2" dia.		3/8"	Dark Dowel	F
*	T7	Rails	2	1/8" dia.		6 3/8"	Maple Dowel	F
	T8	Wheel Shafts	4	1/4" dia.		2 1/4"	Maple Dowel	F
	T9	Hitch Frame	1	1/2"	3/4"	1 1/4"	Maple	F
	T10	Hitch Dowel	1	1/4" dia.		1/2"	Maple Dowel	F
	T11	Main Frame	1	1/4"	2 3/4"	9 5/8"	Oak	F
	T12	Cabin Back	1	1/4"	2 1/4"	2 1/2"	Oak	F
*	T13	Rail Supports	10	1/8"	1/4" dia.		Maple	F
	T14	Axle Block - Front Wheels	1	3/4"	1 1/2"	1 1/2"	Oak	F
	T15	Axle Block - Main Wheels	1	1 1/4"	1 1/2"	4 1/2"	Oak	F
	T16	Hitch	1	1/4"	3/4"	2 1/4"	Maple	R
	T17	Cabin Sides	2	1/4"	2 3/4"	2 3/4"	Oak	R
	T18	Roof	1	3/4"	3"	2 3/4"	Oak	F
	T19	Boiler Bodies	4	1 1/2"	2 1/4"	2 1/4"	Dark Wood	R
	T20	Boiler Divisions	3	1/8"	2 1/4"	2 1/4"	Light Wood	R

Part	Description	Qty.	T	W	L	Material	*
T21	Boiler Cap	1	1/8"	2"	2"	Light Wood	R
T22	Boiler Cover	1	1/8"	1 1/4" dia.		Dark Wood	F
T23	Cylinder Body	1	1 1/4"	1 1/2"	3 3/4"	Oak	R
T24	Front Wheels	2	3/8"	1 1/4" dia.		Maple	F
T25	Main Wheels	6	3/8"	1 3/4" dia.		Maple	F
* T26	Wheel Connectors	2	1/8"	1/2"	4 1/4"	Dark Wood	R
* T27	Connector Shafts	2	1/8"	1/2"	4 1/8"	Dark Wood	R
T28	Deflector	1	1"	1 3/4"	2 1/4"	Pine	F

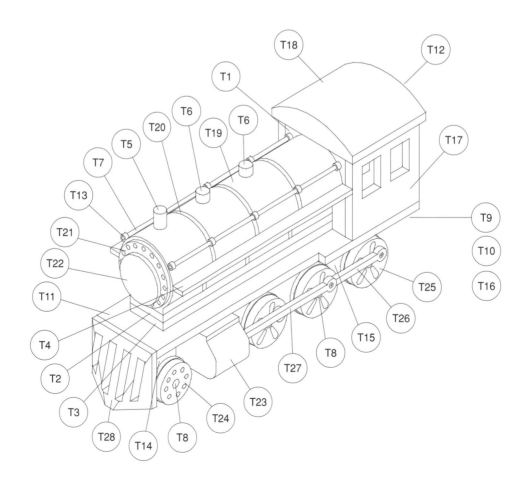

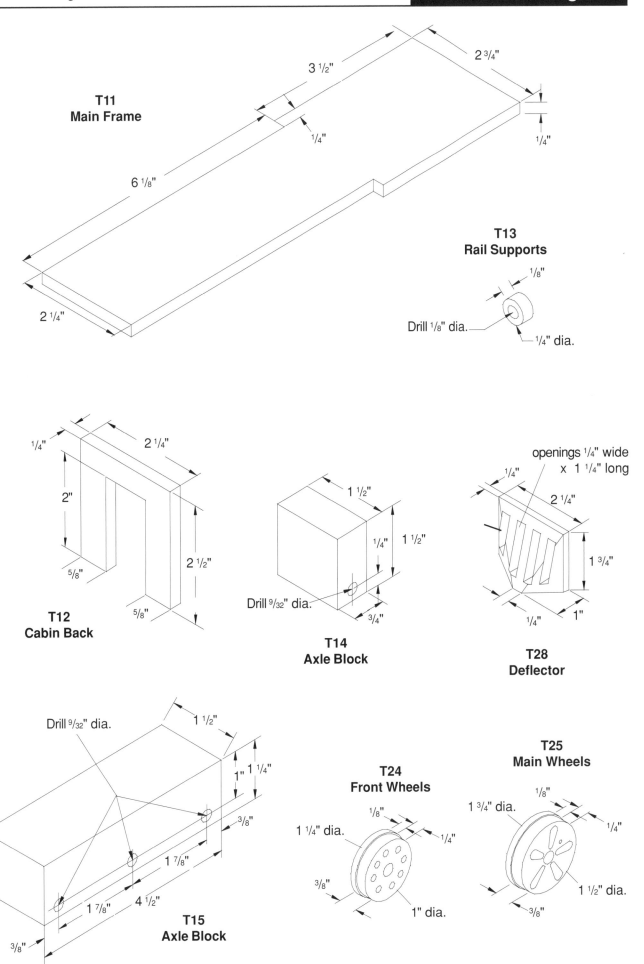

T11
Main Frame

3 1/2"

2 3/4"

1/4"

1/4"

6 1/8"

2 1/4"

T13
Rail Supports

1/8"

Drill 1/8" dia.

1/4" dia.

1/4"

2 1/4"

2"

5/8"

5/8"

2 1/2"

T12
Cabin Back

1 1/2"

1/4"

1 1/2"

Drill 9/32" dia.

3/4"

T14
Axle Block

openings 1/4" wide
x 1 1/4" long

1/4"

2 1/4"

1 3/4"

1/4"

1"

T28
Deflector

T25
Main Wheels

Drill 9/32" dia.

1 1/2"

1" 1 1/4"

3/8"

1 7/8"

1 7/8" 4 1/2"

3/8"

T15
Axle Block

T24
Front Wheels

1/8"

1 1/4" dia.

1/4"

3/8"

1" dia.

1 3/4" dia.

1/8"

1/4"

1 1/2" dia.

3/8"

43

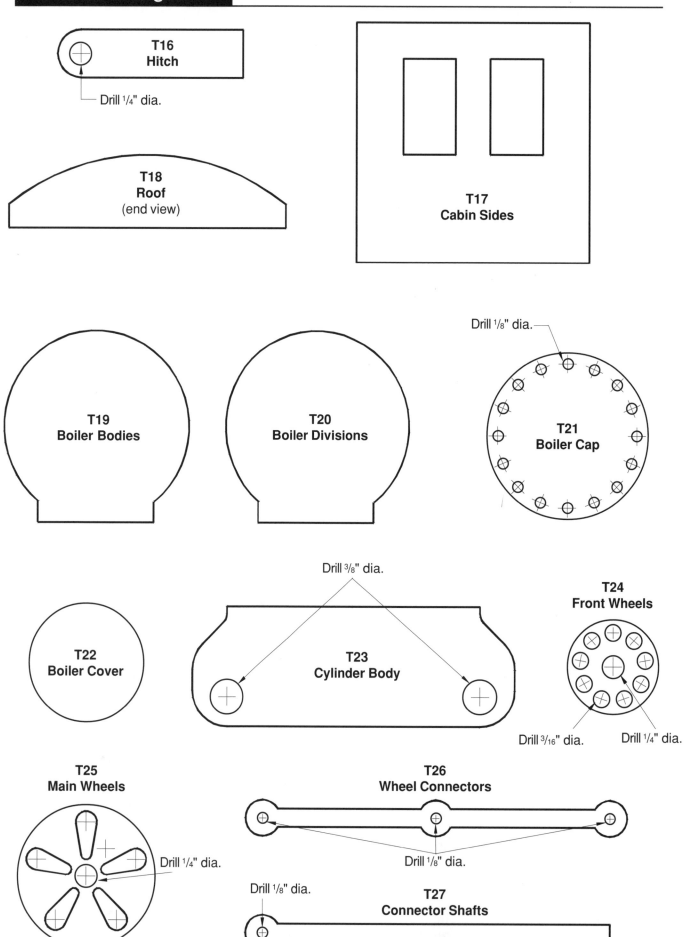

T16
Hitch

Drill ¼" dia.

T18
Roof
(end view)

T17
Cabin Sides

T19
Boiler Bodies

T20
Boiler Divisions

Drill ⅛" dia.

T21
Boiler Cap

T22
Boiler Cover

Drill ⅜" dia.

T23
Cylinder Body

T24
Front Wheels

Drill ³⁄₁₆" dia.   Drill ¼" dia.

T25
Main Wheels

Drill ¼" dia.

T26
Wheel Connectors

Drill ⅛" dia.

Drill ⅛" dia.

T27
Connector Shafts

1

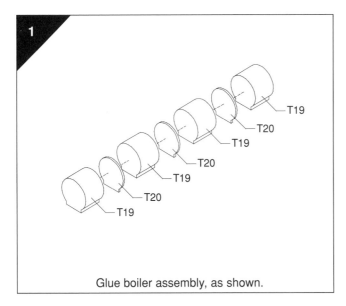

Glue boiler assembly, as shown.

2

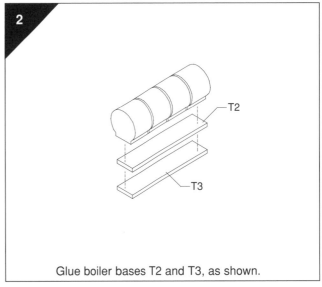

Glue boiler bases T2 and T3, as shown.

3

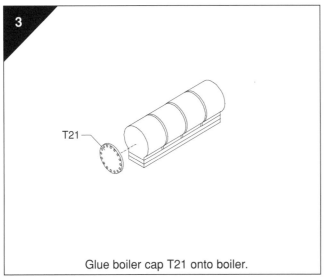

Glue boiler cap T21 onto boiler.

4

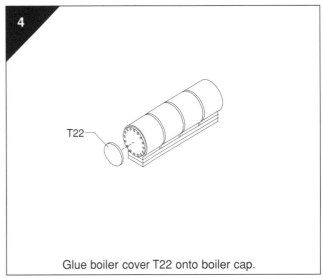

Glue boiler cover T22 onto boiler cap.

5

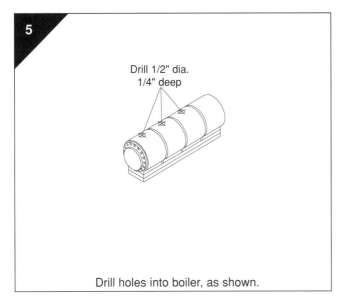

Drill holes into boiler, as shown.

6

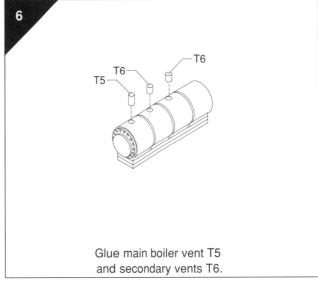

Glue main boiler vent T5
and secondary vents T6.

7

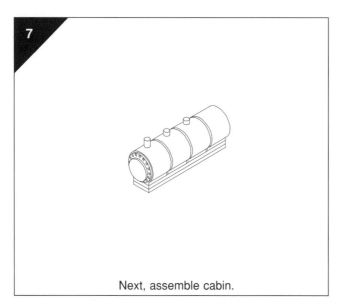

Next, assemble cabin.

8

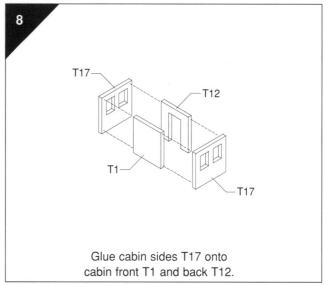

Glue cabin sides T17 onto
cabin front T1 and back T12.

9

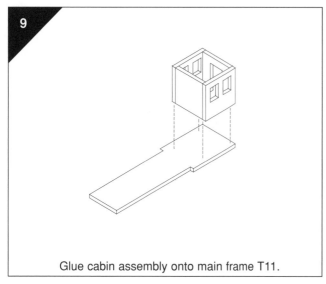

Glue cabin assembly onto main frame T11.

10

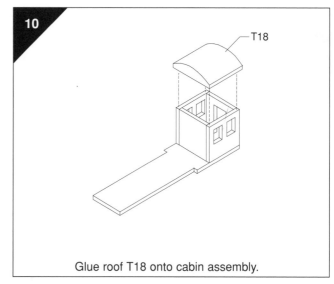

Glue roof T18 onto cabin assembly.

11

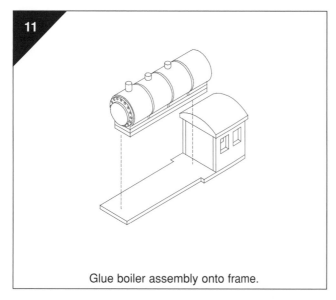

Glue boiler assembly onto frame.

12

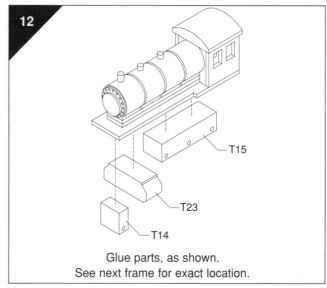

Glue parts, as shown.
See next frame for exact location.

13

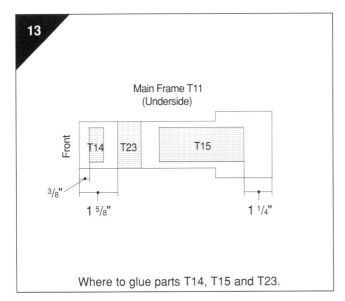

Main Frame T11
(Underside)

Where to glue parts T14, T15 and T23.

14

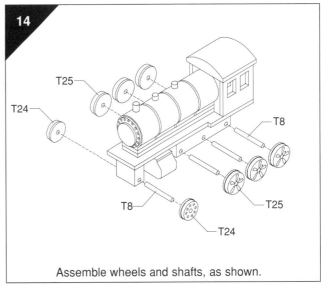

Assemble wheels and shafts, as shown.

15

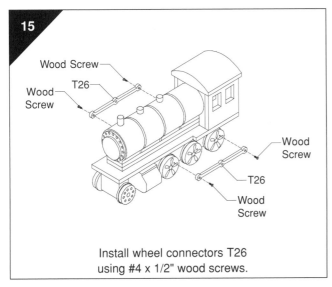

Install wheel connectors T26
using #4 x 1/2" wood screws.

16

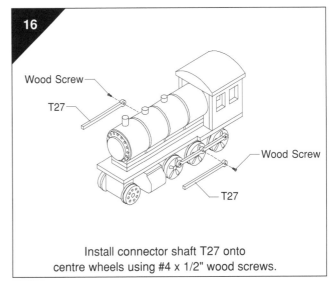

Install connector shaft T27 onto
centre wheels using #4 x 1/2" wood screws.

17

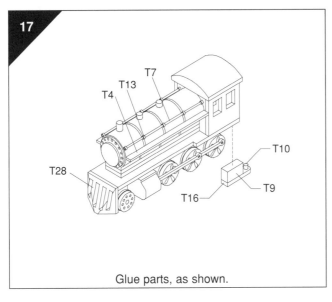

Glue parts, as shown.

18

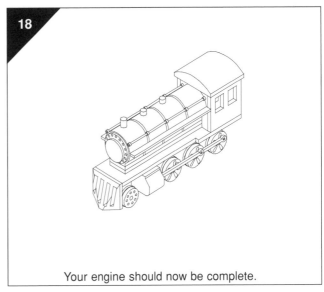

Your engine should now be complete.

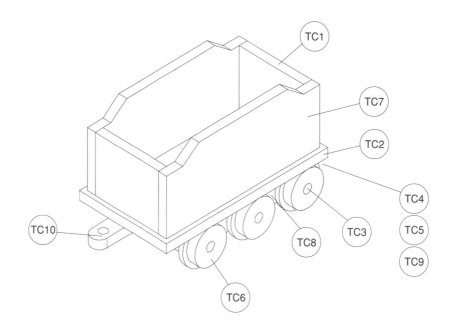

Part	Description	Qty.	T	W	L	Material	*
TC1	End Pieces	2	1/4"	1 5/8"	2"	Oak	F
TC2	Main Frame	1	1/4"	2 3/4"	5"	Oak	F
TC3	Wheel Shafts	3	1/4" dia.		2 1/4"	Maple Dowel	F
TC4	Hitch Frame	1	1/4"	1/2"	1/2"	Maple	F
TC5	Hitch Dowel	1	1/4" dia.		1/2"	Maple Dowel	F
TC6	Wheels	6	3/8"	1 1/4" dia.		Maple	F
TC7	Sides	2	1/4"	2 5/8"	5"	Oak	R
TC8	Axle Block	1	1"	1 1/2"	3 3/4"	Oak	F
TC9	Hitch	1	1/4"	5/8"	1 1/2"	Maple	R
TC10	Hitch	1	1/4"	5/8"	1 3/4"	Maple	R

TC6
Wheels

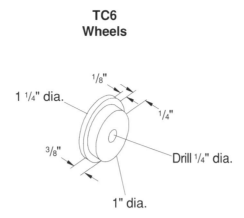

1 ¼" dia.
1/8"
1/4"
3/8"
Drill 1/4" dia.
1" dia.

Full-Sized Patterns: Set One

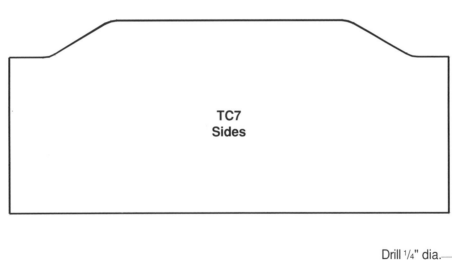

TC7
Sides

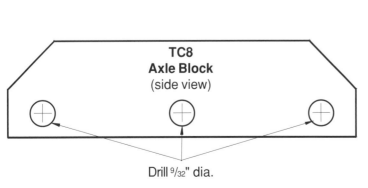

TC8
Axle Block
(side view)

Drill 9/32" dia.

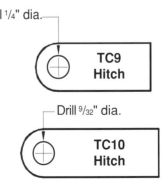

Drill 1/4" dia.

TC9
Hitch

Drill 9/32" dia.

TC10
Hitch

1

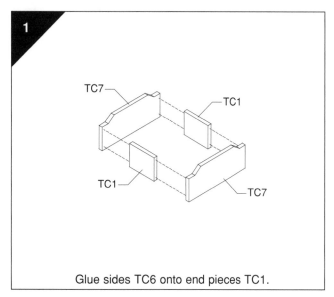

Glue sides TC6 onto end pieces TC1.

2

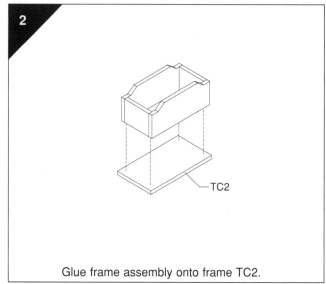

Glue frame assembly onto frame TC2.

3

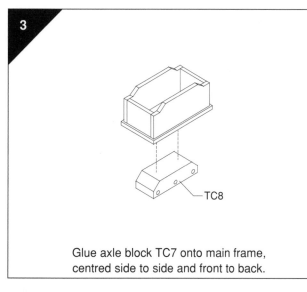

Glue axle block TC7 onto main frame, centred side to side and front to back.

4

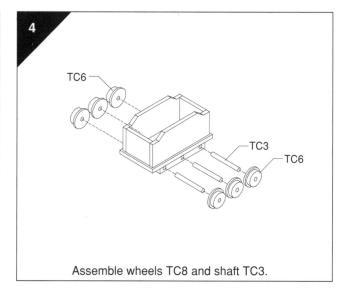

Assemble wheels TC8 and shaft TC3.

5

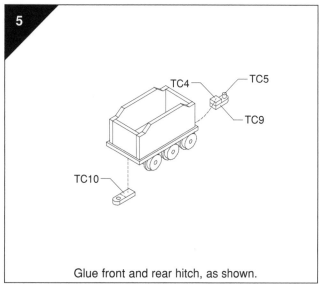

Glue front and rear hitch, as shown.

6

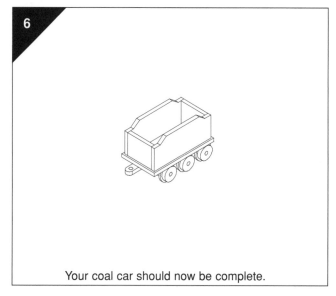

Your coal car should now be complete.

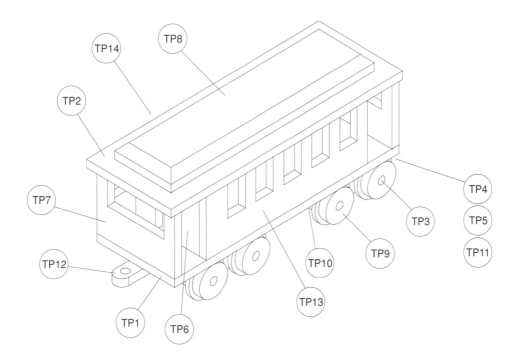

Part	Description	Qty.	T	W	L	Material	*
TP1	Main Frame	1	1/4"	2 3/4"	8"	Oak	F
TP2	First Roof	1	1/4"	3"	8 1/4"	Oak	F
TP3	Wheel Shafts	4	1/4" dia.		2 1/4"	Maple Dowel	F
TP4	Hitch Frame	1	1/4"	1/2"	1/2"	Maple	F
TP5	Hitch Dowel	1	1/4" dia.		1/2"	Maple Dowel	F
TP6	Cabin Back & Front	2	1/4"	2 1/4"	2 1/4"	Oak	F
TP7	Ends	2	1/4"	2 3/4"	2 1/4"	Oak	F
TP8	Second Roof	1	1/2"	2"	7 1/4"	Oak	F
TP9	Wheels	8	3/8"	1 1/4" dia.		Maple	F
TP10	Axle Blocks	2	1"	1 1/2"	2 1/4"	Oak	F
TP11	Hitch	1	1/4"	5/8"	1 1/2"	Maple	R
TP12	Hitch	1	1/4"	5/8"	1 3/4"	Maple	R
TP13	Cabin Side	1	1/4"	2 1/2"	6"	Oak	R
TP14	Cabin Side	1	1/4"	2 1/2"	7 3/4"	Oak	R

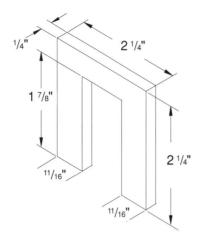

TP6
Cabin Back & Front

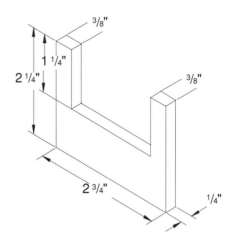

TP7
Ends

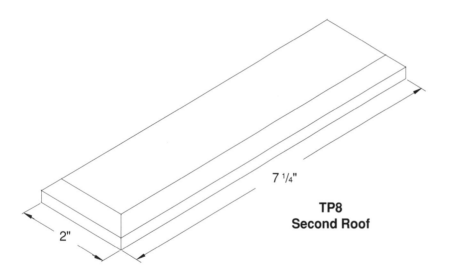

TP8
Second Roof

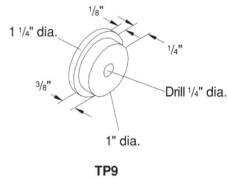

TP9
Wheels

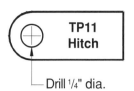

TP11
Hitch

Drill ¼" dia.

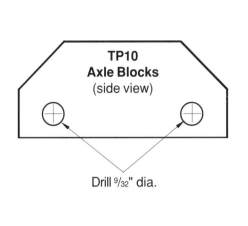

TP10
Axle Blocks
(side view)

Drill 9/32" dia.

TP12
Hitch

Drill 9/32" dia.

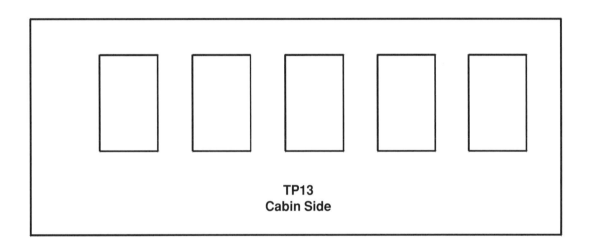

TP13
Cabin Side

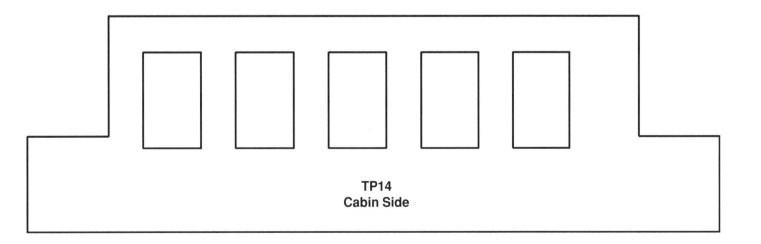

TP14
Cabin Side

1

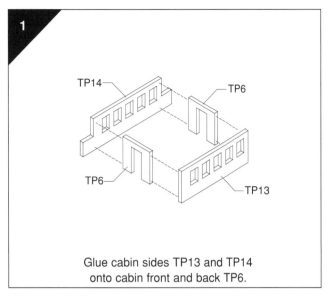

Glue cabin sides TP13 and TP14
onto cabin front and back TP6.

2

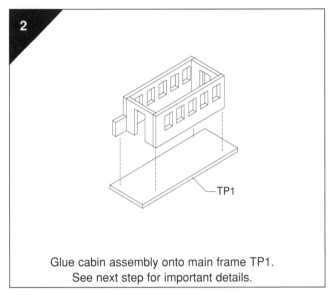

Glue cabin assembly onto main frame TP1.
See next step for important details.

3

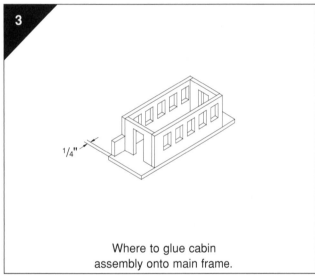

Where to glue cabin
assembly onto main frame.

4

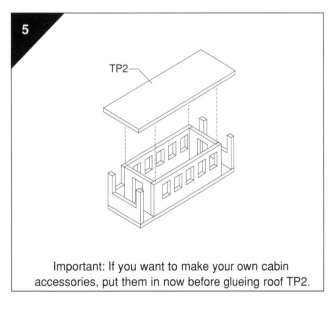

Glue ends TP7, as shown.

5

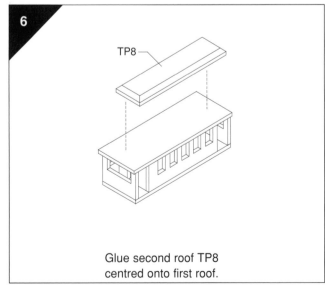

Important: If you want to make your own cabin
accessories, put them in now before glueing roof TP2.

6

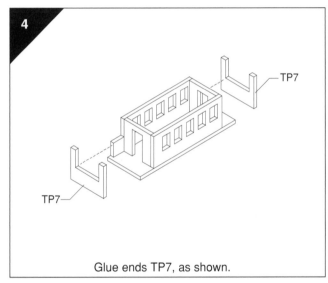

Glue second roof TP8
centred onto first roof.

7

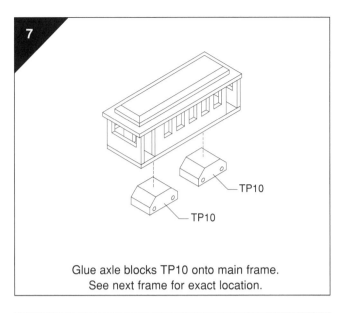

Glue axle blocks TP10 onto main frame.
See next frame for exact location.

8

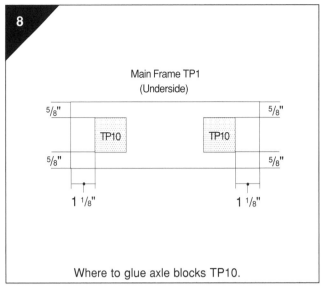

Where to glue axle blocks TP10.

9

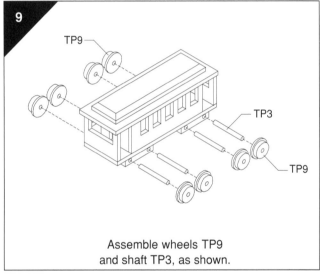

Assemble wheels TP9
and shaft TP3, as shown.

10

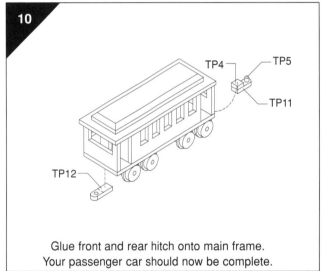

Glue front and rear hitch onto main frame.
Your passenger car should now be complete.

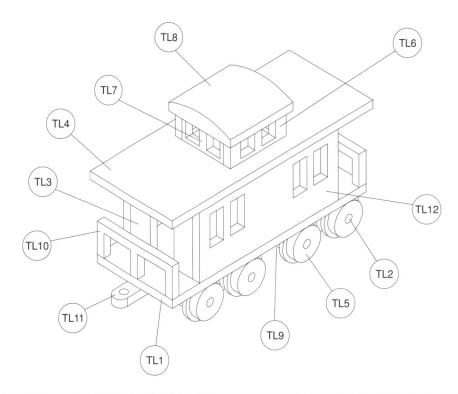

Part	Description	Qty.	T	W	L	Material	*
TL1	Main Frame	1	1/4"	2 3/4"	7"	Oak	F
TL2	Wheel Shafts	4	1/4" dia.		2 1/4"	Maple Dowel	F
TL3	Cabin Back & Front	2	1/4"	2 1/4"	2 1/4"	Oak	F
TL4	First Roof	1	1/4"	3"	7 1/4"	Oak	F
TL5	Wheels	8	3/8"	1 1/4" dia.		Maple	F
TL6	Second Cabin Sides	2	1/4"	1"	2 1/4"	Oak	R
TL7	Second Cabin Back & Front	2	1/4"	1"	1 3/4"	Oak	R
TL8	Second Cabin Roof	1	1/2"	2 1/4"	2 1/4"	Oak	F
TL9	Axle Blocks	2	1"	1 1/2"	2 1/4"	Oak	F
TL10	Railings	2	1/4"	1 1/4"	3"	Oak	R
TL11	Hitch	1	1/4"	5/8"	1 3/4"	Maple	R
TL12	Cabin Sides	2	1/4"	2 1/2"	5 1/4"	Oak	R

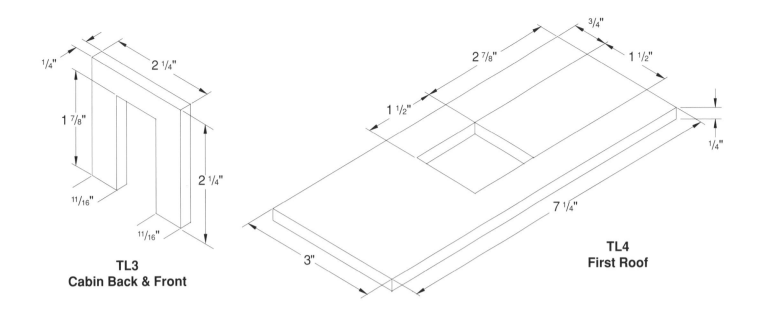

TL3
Cabin Back & Front

TL4
First Roof

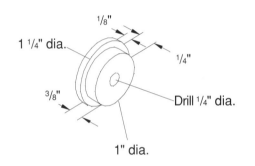

TL5
Wheels

1 1/4" dia.

1/8"

1/4"

3/8"

Drill 1/4" dia.

1" dia.

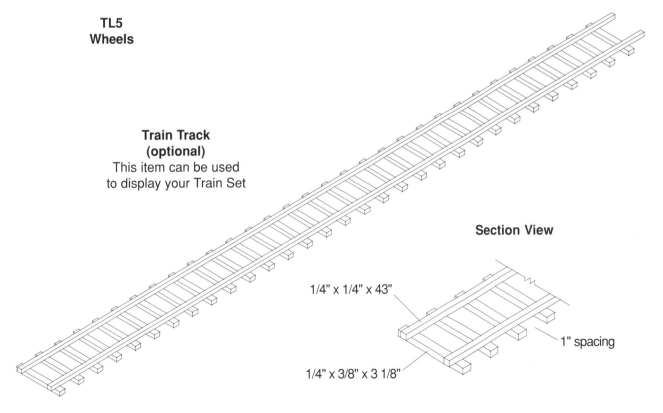

Train Track
(optional)
This item can be used
to display your Train Set

Section View

1/4" x 1/4" x 43"

1" spacing

1/4" x 3/8" x 3 1/8"

TL6
Secondary Cabin Sides

TL7
Second Cabin Back & Front

TL8
Second Cabin Roof
(end view)

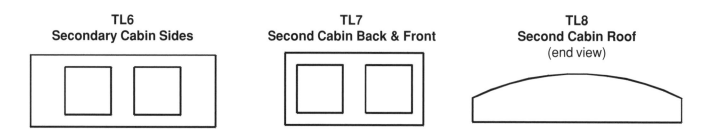

TL9
Axle Block
(side view)

TL10
Railings

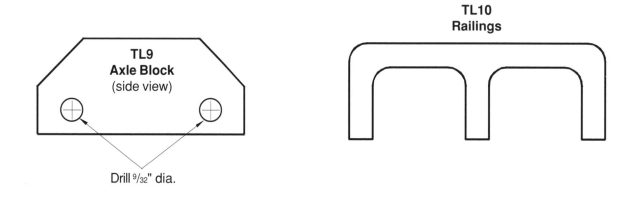

Drill ⁹/₃₂" dia.

TL11
Hitch

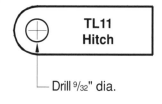

Drill ⁹/₃₂" dia.

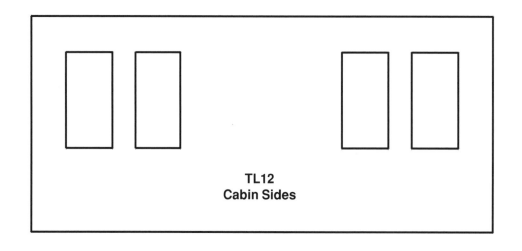

TL12
Cabin Sides

1

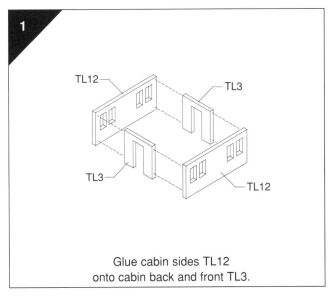

Glue cabin sides TL12
onto cabin back and front TL3.

2

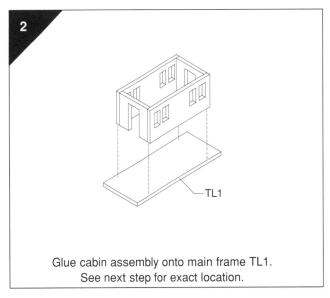

Glue cabin assembly onto main frame TL1.
See next step for exact location.

3

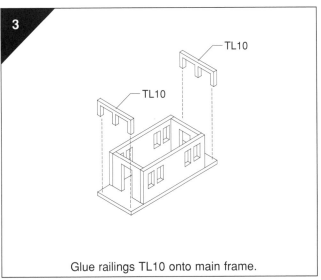

Glue railings TL10 onto main frame.

4

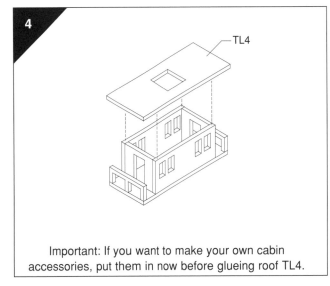

Important: If you want to make your own cabin
accessories, put them in now before glueing roof TL4.

5

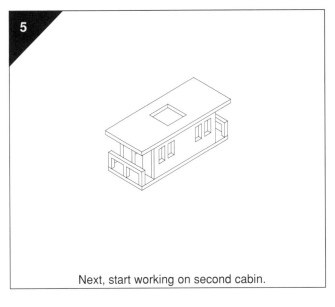

Next, start working on second cabin.

6

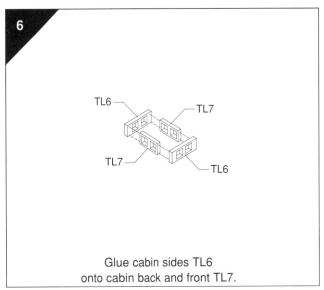

Glue cabin sides TL6
onto cabin back and front TL7.

7

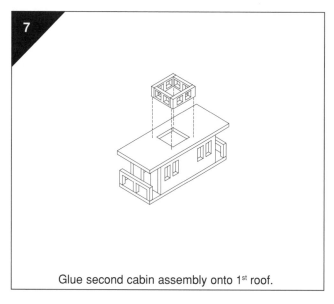

Glue second cabin assembly onto 1st roof.

8

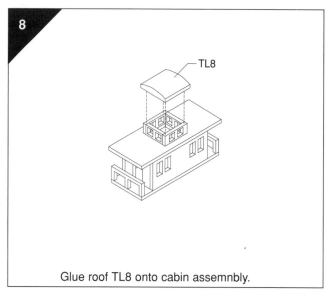

TL8

Glue roof TL8 onto cabin assemnbly.

9

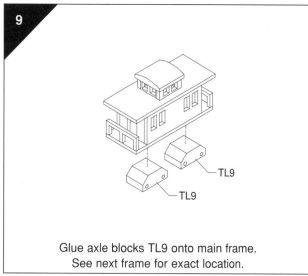

TL9

TL9

Glue axle blocks TL9 onto main frame.
See next frame for exact location.

10

Main Frame TP1
(Underside)

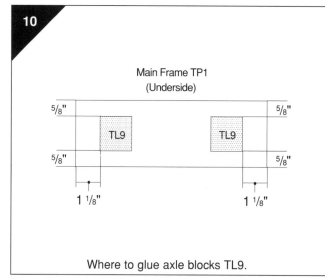

$5/8"$ $5/8"$

TL9   TL9

$5/8"$ $5/8"$

$1 \, 1/8"$ $1 \, 1/8"$

Where to glue axle blocks TL9.

11

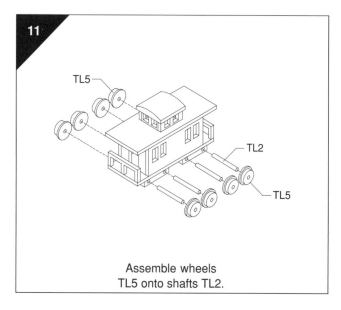

TL5

TL2

TL5

Assemble wheels
TL5 onto shafts TL2.

12

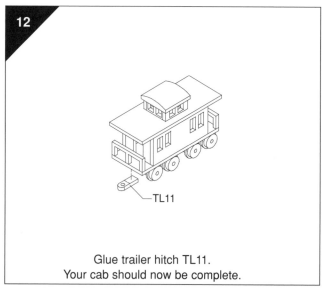

TL11

Glue trailer hitch TL11.
Your cab should now be complete.

18 WHEELER

Step 1   Start by cutting materials needed using the List of Materials on pages 64 and 65. **Pay attention to the rough and finished size, and identify parts as they are cut.**

Please note: Different types of wood can be used for the various parts. It is suggested, however, that hard wood be used since many of the parts would be much too fragile if using soft wood. We have used a combination of Maple, Pine, Oak and exotic woods such as Padauk (dark wood), Yellowheart (light colour) and Mahogany (dark wood) to give the models a nice contrast!

Step 2   Parts B1 to B18 are already complete. Parts B19 to B26 will need a few more steps. See the Parts Drawing section on page 66 for more details.

Step 3   Parts B27 to B34 require removing the Full-Sized Patterns sheet found on page 115 of the Appendix. Cut out the patterns, leaving approximately $1/16$" all around, and place on the proper piece of wood. Patterns can be secured to the wood using either spray adhesive or rubber cement. If using the latter, cut and sand the part first to finished size. If drilling is required, mark the hole by inserting an awl or nail through the pattern into the wood. Remove the pattern before drilling.

Step 4   Follow the assembly drawings on pages 68 to 70 to complete your model.

Please note: In order for this model to move properly, it is recommended that you apply a lubricant to wheel shafts and axle block holes. Lard is the cheapest and safest option. It is non-toxic and found in most households.

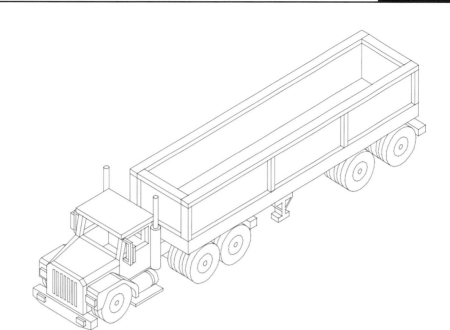

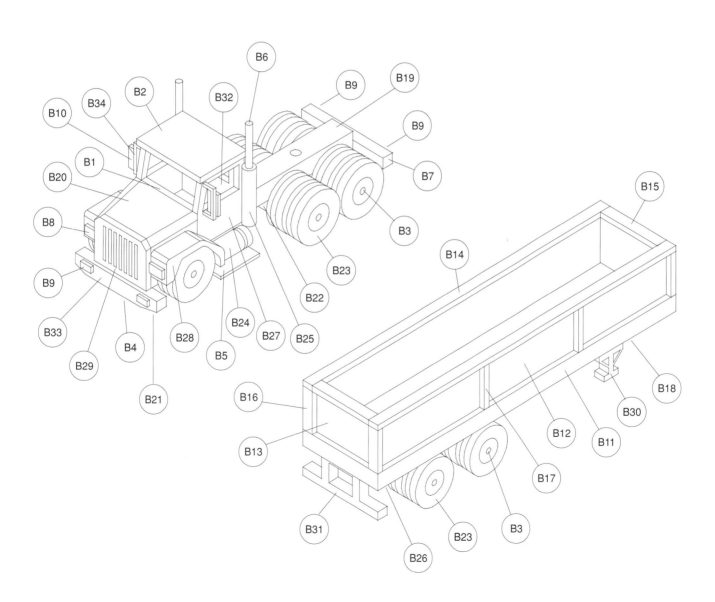

Part	Description	Qty.	T	W	L	Material	*
B1	Cabin Front	1	1/4"	1 3/8"	2 1/2"	Oak	F
B2	Roof	1	1/4"	3 1/8"	2 1/4"	Oak	F
B3	Wheel Shafts	5	3/8" dia.		3 3/4"	Maple Dowel	F
B4	Bumper Support	1	3/4"	3/4"	1 1/2"	Maple	F
B5	Floor Boards	2	1/8"	3/4"	1 7/8"	Dark Wood	F
* B6	Muffler - Top Pieces	2	1/4" dia.		2"	Maple Dowel	F
B7	Rear Bumper	1	1/4"	3/8"	4"	Oak	F
* B8	Headlights	2	1/8"	3/8"	5/8"	Light Colour	F
* B9	Flashers & Brake Lights	4	1/8"	1/4"	1/2"	Dark Wood	F
* B10	Mirrors	2	1/8"	1/2"	1"	Dark Wood	F
B11	Trailer Frame	1	3/4"	4"	16"	Maple	F
B12	Trailer Sides	2	1/4"	2 1/4"	15 1/2"	Oak	F
B13	Trailer Back & Front	2	1/4"	2 1/4"	3"	Oak	F
B14	Top Frames	2	1/4"	1/2"	16"	Maple	F
B15	Top Frames	2	1/4"	1/2"	3"	Maple	F
B16	End Braces	4	1/4"	1/2"	2 1/4"	Maple	F
B17	Braces	4	1/4"	1/4"	2 1/4"	Maple	F
B18	Trailer Hitch	1	3/8" dia.		7/8"	Maple Dowel	F
B19	Main Frame	1	3/4"	2 1/2"	10 1/2"	Maple	F
B20	Hood	1	1 3/8"	3"	2 1/4"	Oak	F

Part	Description	Qty.	T	W	L	Material	*
B21	Axle Block - Front Wheels	1	1"	1"	2 1/2"	Maple	F
B22	Axle Blocks - Rear Wheels	2	1"	1"	1"	Maple	F
B23	Wheels	18	3/4"	2" dia.		Maple	F
B24	Fuel Tanks	2	3/4" dia.		1 7/8"	Maple Dowel	F
* B25	Muffler - Bottom Pieces	2	1/2" dia.		2 1/4"	Maple Dowel	F
B26	Trailer Axle Block	1	1"	1 7/8"	3 1/8"	Maple	F
B27	Cabin Sides	2	1/4"	2 7/8"	2 1/2"	Oak	R
B28	Fenders	2	3/4"	2"	2 7/8"	Oak	R
B29	Front Grill	1	1/4"	2 3/4"	2 1/4"	Maple	R
* B30	Trailer Supports	2	1/2"	1 1/2"	1 1/2"	Maple	R
B31	Trailer Bumper	1	1/2"	1 1/2"	4 1/4"	Maple	R
B32	Cabin Back	1	1/4"	2 3/4"	2 7/8"	Oak	R
B33	Front Bumper	1	1/2"	1"	4 1/4"	Oak	R
* B34	Mirror Supports	2	1/8"	3/4"	1 1/2"	Maple	R

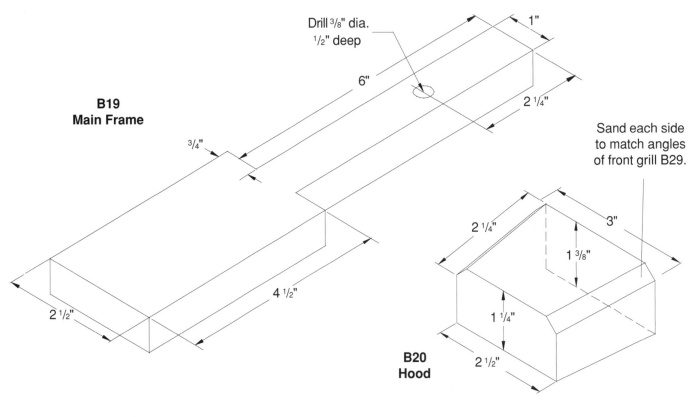

B19
Main Frame

Drill 3/8" dia.
1/2" deep

6"

1"

2 1/4"

3/4"

2 1/2"

4 1/2"

Sand each side
to match angles
of front grill B29.

2 1/4"

3"

1 3/8"

1 1/4"

2 1/2"

B20
Hood

B23
Wheels

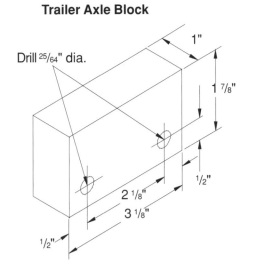

3/4"

Drill 3/8" dia.

Drill 7/8" dia.
5/16" deep

2" dia.

B21
Axle Blocks - Front Wheels

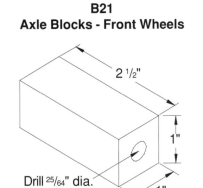

2 1/2"

1"

Drill 25/64" dia.

1"

B22
Axle Blocks - Rear Wheels

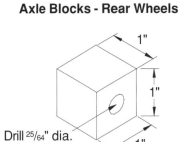

1"

1"

Drill 25/64" dia.

1"

B25
Muffler- Bottom Pieces

Drill 1/4" dia.
5/8" deep

2 1/4"

1/2" dia.

B26
Trailer Axle Block

Drill 25/64" dia.

1"

1 7/8"

1/2"

2 1/8"

3 1/8"

1/2"

B24
Fuel Tanks

1/4"

Groove 1/16" wide
1/16" deep

1/4"

3/4" dia.

1 7/8"

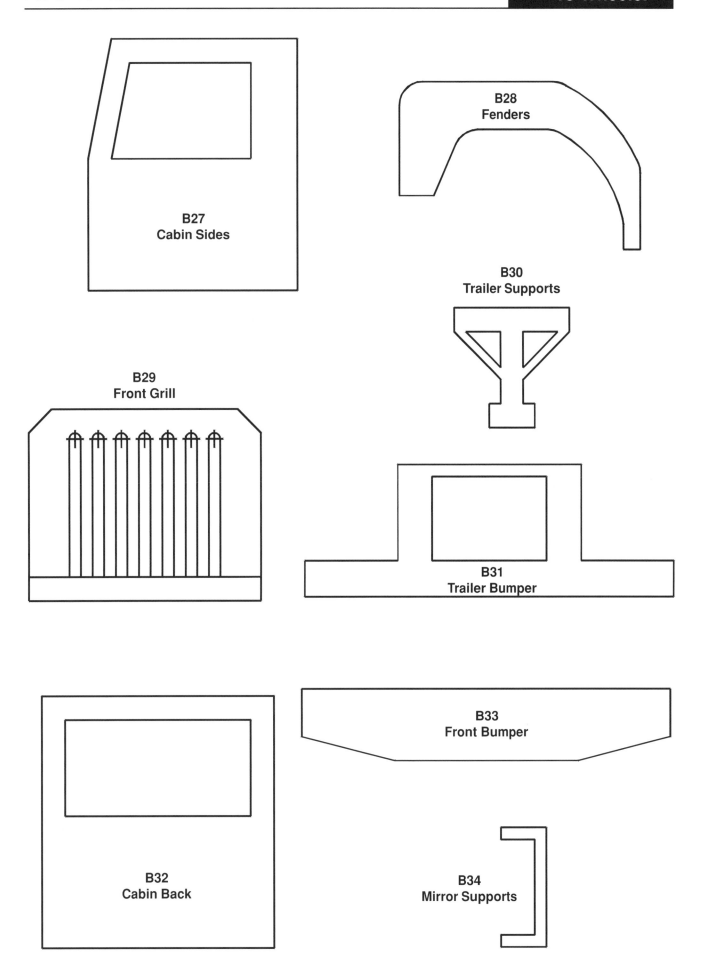

B28
Fenders

B27
Cabin Sides

B30
Trailer Supports

B29
Front Grill

B31
Trailer Bumper

B33
Front Bumper

B32
Cabin Back

B34
Mirror Supports

1

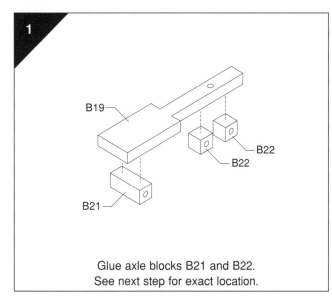

Glue axle blocks B21 and B22.
See next step for exact location.

2

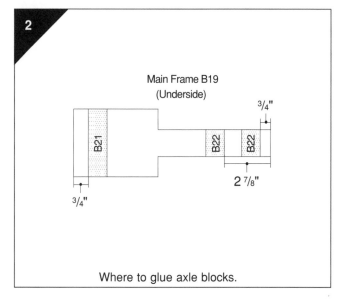

Main Frame B19
(Underside)

Where to glue axle blocks.

3

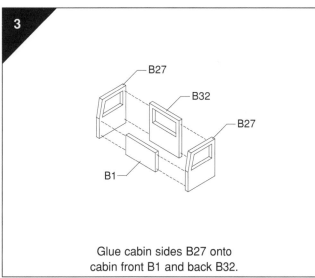

Glue cabin sides B27 onto
cabin front B1 and back B32.

4

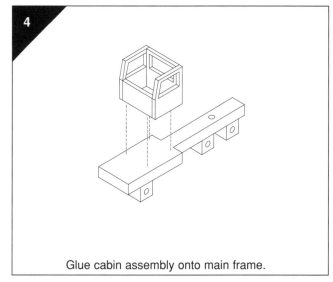

Glue cabin assembly onto main frame.

5

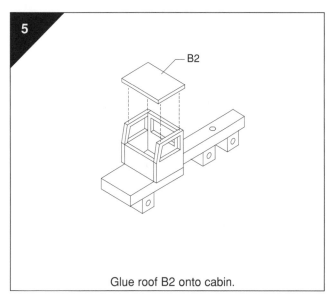

Glue roof B2 onto cabin.

6

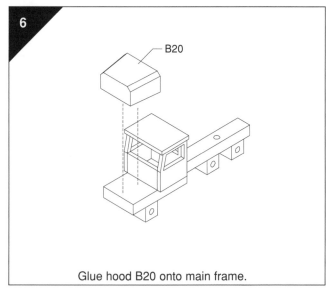

Glue hood B20 onto main frame.

7

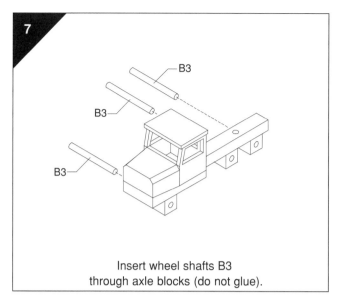

Insert wheel shafts B3
through axle blocks (do not glue).

8

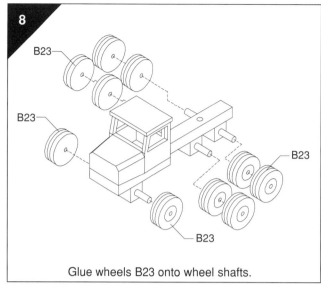

Glue wheels B23 onto wheel shafts.

9

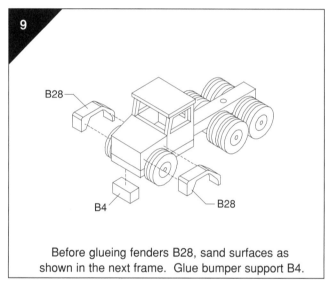

Before glueing fenders B28, sand surfaces as
shown in the next frame. Glue bumper support B4.

10

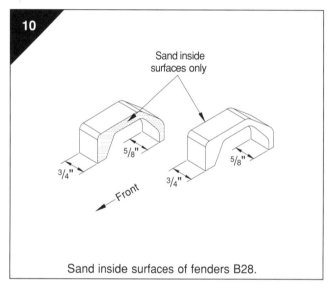

Sand inside surfaces of fenders B28.

11

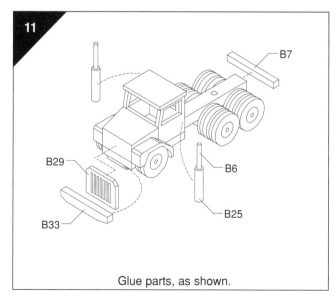

Glue parts, as shown.

12

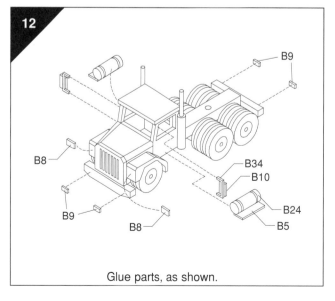

Glue parts, as shown.

13

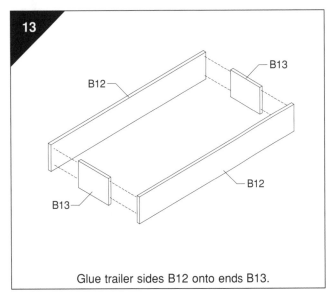

Glue trailer sides B12 onto ends B13.

14

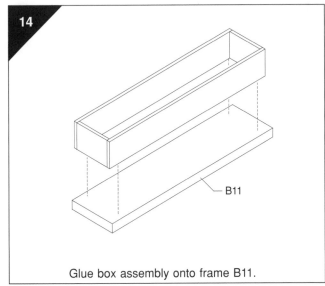

Glue box assembly onto frame B11.

15

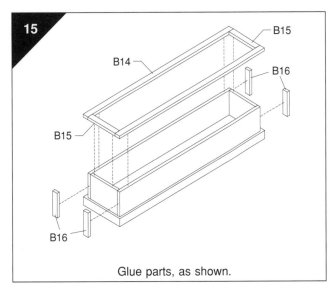

Glue parts, as shown.

16

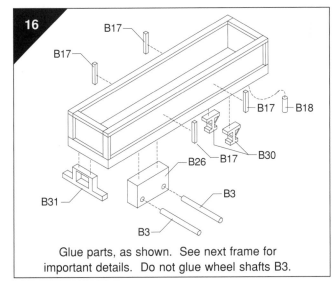

Glue parts, as shown. See next frame for important details. Do not glue wheel shafts B3.

17

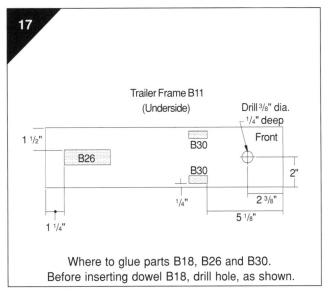

Trailer Frame B11
(Underside)

Drill ³/₈" dia.
¹/₄" deep
Front

B30

1 ¹/₂"

B26

B30

2"

¹/₄"

2 ³/₈"

5 ¹/₈"

1 ¹/₄"

Where to glue parts B18, B26 and B30.
Before inserting dowel B18, drill hole, as shown.

18

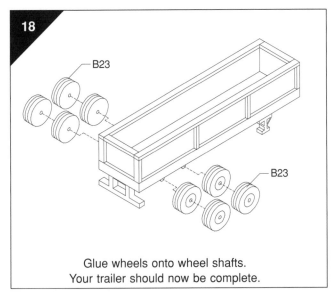

Glue wheels onto wheel shafts.
Your trailer should now be complete.

DUMP TRUCK

Step 1   Start by cutting materials needed using the List of Materials on pages 74 and 75. **Pay attention to the rough and finished size, and identify parts as they are cut.**

Please note: Different types of wood can be used for the various parts. It is suggested, however, that hard wood be used since many of the parts would be much too fragile if using soft wood. We have used a combination of Maple, Pine, Oak and exotic woods such as Padauk (dark wood), Yellowheart (light colour) and Mahogany (dark wood) to give the models a nice contrast!

Step 2   Parts D1 to D17 are already complete. Parts D18 to D26 will need a few more steps. See the Parts Drawing section on page 76 for more details.

Step 3   Parts D27 to D37 require removing the Full-Sized Patterns sheet found on page 117 of the Appendix. Cut out the patterns, leaving approximately $1/16$" all around, and place on the proper piece of wood. Patterns can be secured to the wood using either spray adhesive or rubber cement. If using the latter, cut and sand the part first to finished size. If drilling is required, mark the hole by inserting an awl or nail through the pattern into the wood. Remove the pattern before drilling.

Step 4   Follow the assembly drawings on pages 78 to 81 to complete your model.

Please note: In order for this model to move properly, it is recommended that you apply a lubricant to wheel shafts and axle block holes. Lard is the cheapest and safest option. It is non-toxic and found in most households.

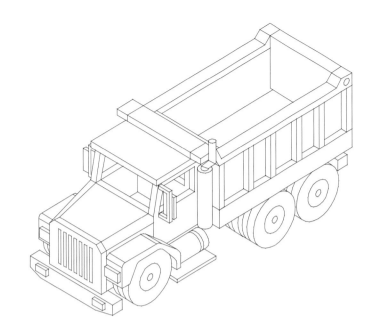

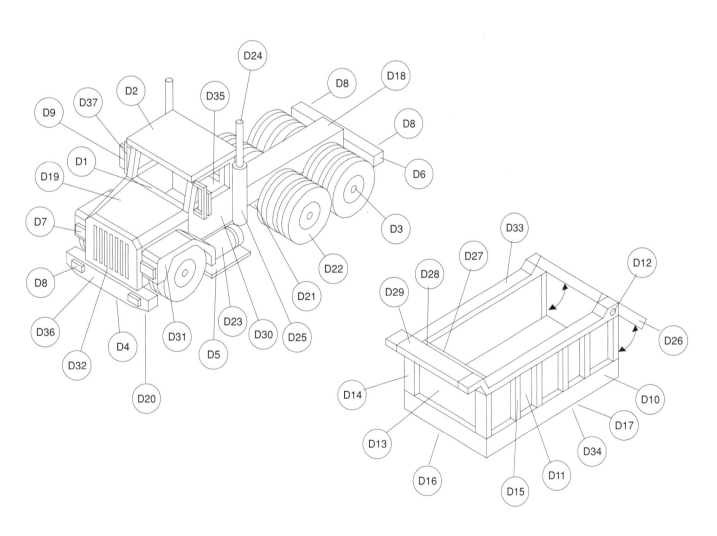

Part	Description	Qty.	T	W	L	Material	*
D1	Cabin Front	1	1/4"	1 3/8"	2 1/2"	Oak	F
D2	Roof	1	1/4"	3 1/8"	2 1/4"	Oak	F
D3	Wheel Shafts	3	3/8" dia.		3 3/4"	Maple Dowel	F
D4	Bumper Support	1	3/4"	3/4"	1 1/2"	Maple	F
D5	Floor Boards	2	1/8"	3/4"	1 7/8"	Dark Wood	F
D6	Rear Bumper	1	1/4"	3/8"	4"	Oak	F
* D7	Headlights	2	1/8"	3/8"	5/8"	Light Colour	F
* D8	Flashers & Brake Lights	4	1/8"	1/4"	1/2"	Dark Wood	F
* D9	Mirrors	2	1/8"	1/2"	1"	Dark Wood	F
D10	Box Frame	1	3/4"	4"	6 1/2"	Maple	F
D11	Box Sides	2	1/4"	1 3/4"	6"	Oak	F
D12	Gate Shaft	1	1/4" dia.		4"	Maple Dowel	F
D13	Box Front	1	1/4"	1 3/4"	3"	Oak	F
D14	End Braces	4	1/4"	1/2"	1 3/4"	Maple	F
D15	Braces	8	1/4"	1/4"	1 3/4"	Maple	F
D16	Pivot Frame	1	1/8"	1 1/16"	5 3/4"	Maple	F
D17	Pivot Shaft	1	1/4" dia.		1 9/16"	Maple Dowel	F
D18	Main Frame	1	3/4"	2 1/2"	10 1/2"	Maple	F
D19	Hood	1	1 3/8"	3"	2 1/4"	Oak	F
D20	Axle Block - Front Wheels	1	1"	1"	2 1/2"	Maple	F

Part	Description	Qty.	T	W	L	Material	*
D21	Axle Block - Rear Wheels	2	1"	1"	1"	Maple	F
D22	Wheels	10	3/4"	2" dia.		Maple	F
D23	Fuel Tanks	2	3/4" dia.		1 7/8"	Maple Dowel	F
D24	Muffler - Top Parts	1	See parts drawing			Maple Dowel	F
D25	Muffler - Bottom Piece	1	1/2" dia.		2 1/4"	Maple Dowel	F
D26	Gate Door	1	1/2"	2 1/8"	2 7/8"	Oak	F
D27	Box Frame - Part 1 of 3	1	1/4"	3/4"	3"	Maple	F
D28	Box Frame - Part 2 of 3	1	1/4"	5/8"	3"	Maple	F
D29	Box Frame - Part 3 of 3	1	1/4"	7/8"	3"	Maple	F
D30	Cabin Sides	2	1/4"	2 7/8"	2 1/2"	Oak	R
D31	Fenders	2	3/4"	2"	2 7/8"	Oak	R
D32	Front Grill	1	1/4"	2 3/4"	2 1/4"	Maple	R
D33	Box Frames	2	1/2"	1"	7 5/8"	Maple	R
D34	Pivot Sides	2	1/4"	1"	6"	Maple	R
D35	Cabin Back	1	1/4"	2 3/4"	2 7/8"	Oak	R
D36	Front Bumper	1	1/2"	1"	4 1/4"	Oak	R
D37	Mirror Supports	2	1/8"	3/4"	1 1/2"	Maple	R

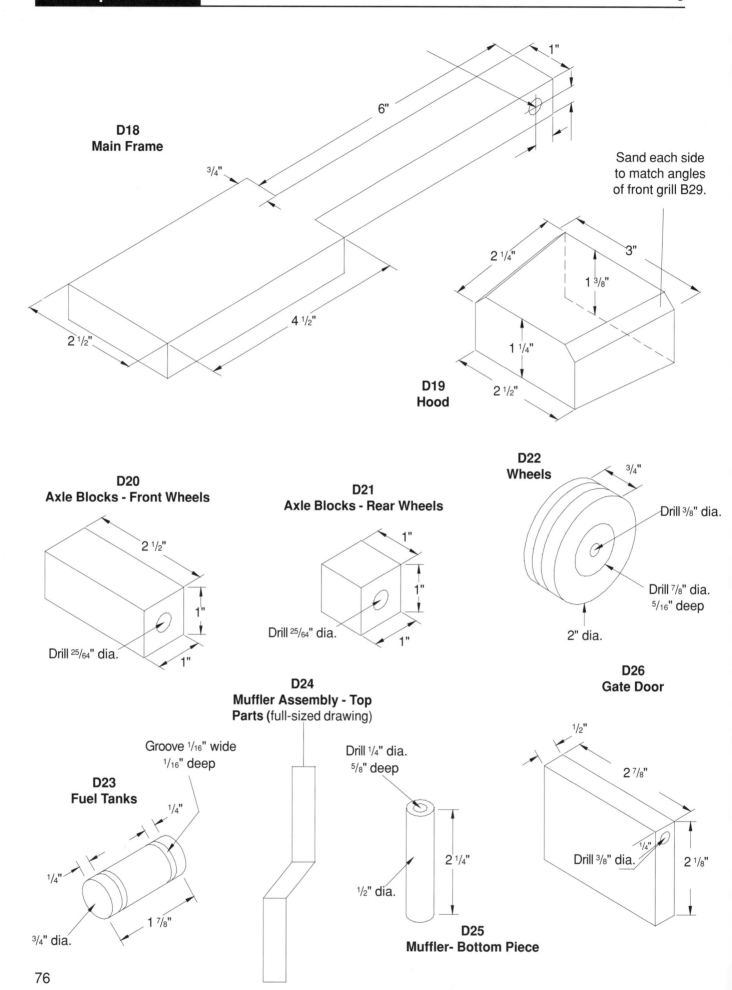

D18
Main Frame

6"

1"

3/4"

4 1/2"

2 1/2"

Sand each side
to match angles
of front grill B29.

2 1/4"

3"

1 3/8"

1 1/4"

2 1/2"

D19
Hood

D20
Axle Blocks - Front Wheels

2 1/2"

1"

1"

Drill 25/64" dia.

D21
Axle Blocks - Rear Wheels

1"

1"

1"

Drill 25/64" dia.

D22
Wheels

3/4"

Drill 3/8" dia.

Drill 7/8" dia.
5/16" deep

2" dia.

D23
Fuel Tanks

Groove 1/16" wide
1/16" deep

1/4"

1/4"

3/4" dia.

1 7/8"

D24
Muffler Assembly - Top
Parts (full-sized drawing)

Drill 1/4" dia.
5/8" deep

1/2" dia.

2 1/4"

D25
Muffler- Bottom Piece

D26
Gate Door

1/2"

2 7/8"

1/4"

Drill 3/8" dia.

2 1/8"

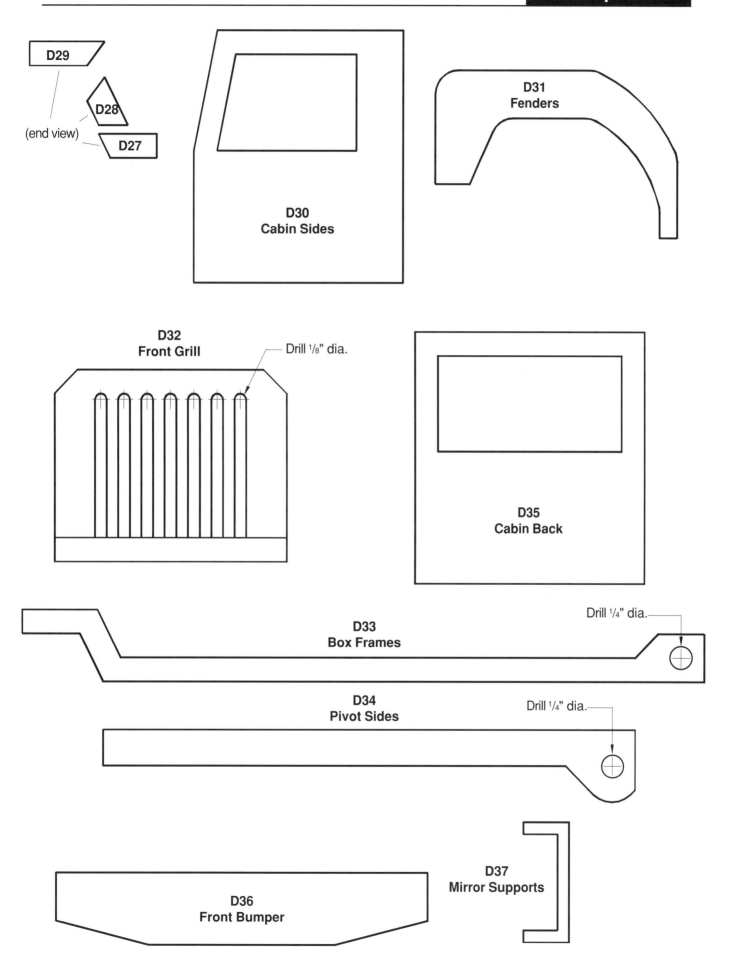

D29

D28

D27

(end view)

**D30
Cabin Sides**

**D31
Fenders**

**D32
Front Grill**

Drill ¹/₈" dia.

**D35
Cabin Back**

**D33
Box Frames**

Drill ¹/₄" dia.

**D34
Pivot Sides**

Drill ¹/₄" dia.

**D37
Mirror Supports**

**D36
Front Bumper**

1

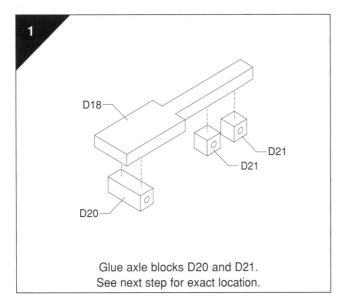

Glue axle blocks D20 and D21.
See next step for exact location.

2

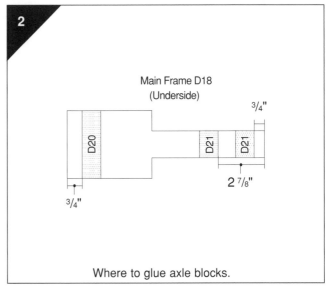

Where to glue axle blocks.

3

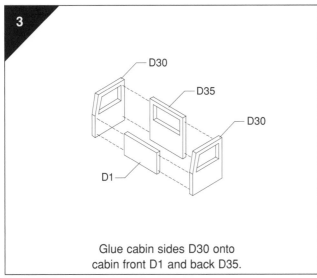

Glue cabin sides D30 onto
cabin front D1 and back D35.

4

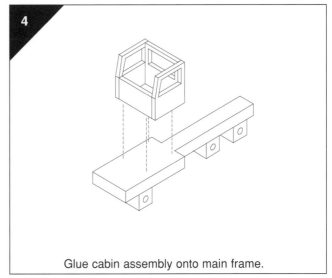

Glue cabin assembly onto main frame.

5

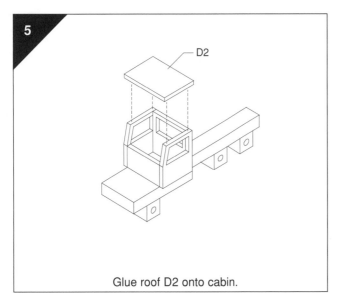

Glue roof D2 onto cabin.

6

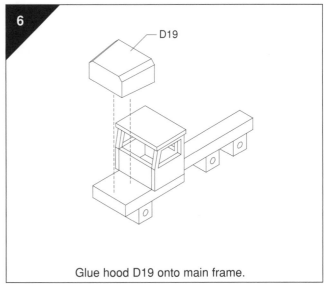

Glue hood D19 onto main frame.

7

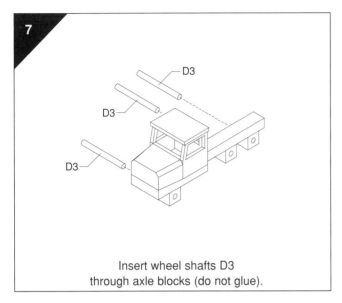

Insert wheel shafts D3
through axle blocks (do not glue).

8

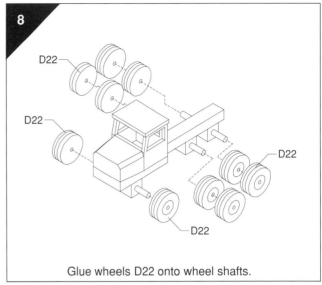

Glue wheels D22 onto wheel shafts.

9

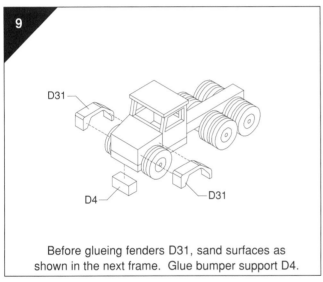

Before glueing fenders D31, sand surfaces as
shown in the next frame. Glue bumper support D4.

10

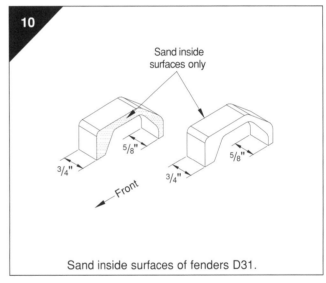

Sand inside surfaces of fenders D31.

11

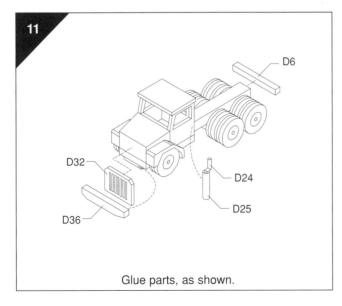

Glue parts, as shown.

12

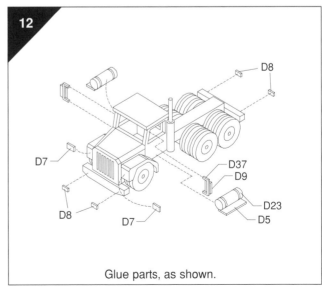

Glue parts, as shown.

13

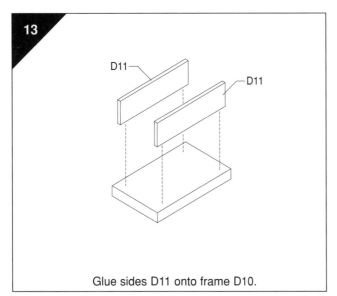

Glue sides D11 onto frame D10.

14

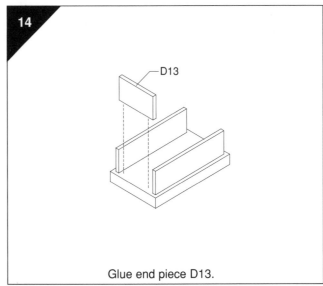

Glue end piece D13.

15

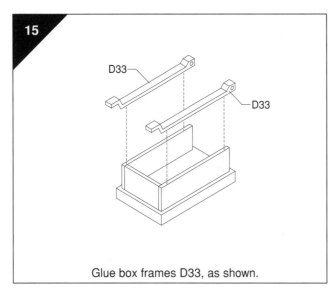

Glue box frames D33, as shown.

16

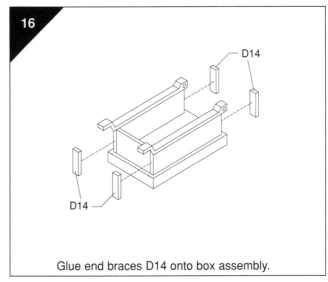

Glue end braces D14 onto box assembly.

17

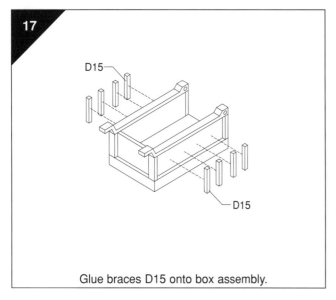

Glue braces D15 onto box assembly.

18

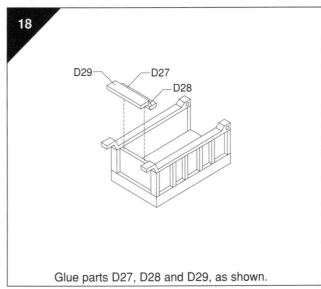

Glue parts D27, D28 and D29, as shown.

19

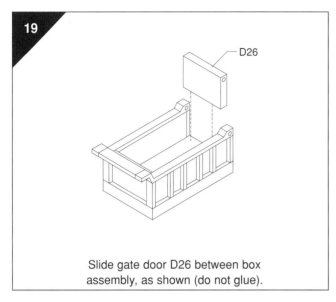

Slide gate door D26 between box
assembly, as shown (do not glue).

20

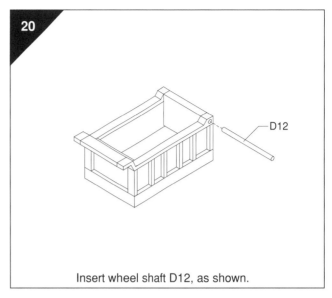

Insert wheel shaft D12, as shown.

21

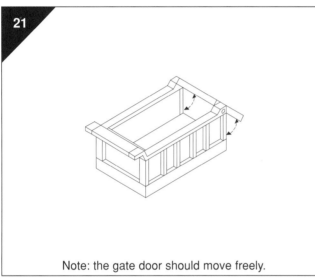

Note: the gate door should move freely.

22

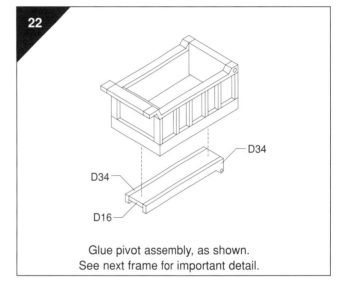

Glue pivot assembly, as shown.
See next frame for important detail.

23

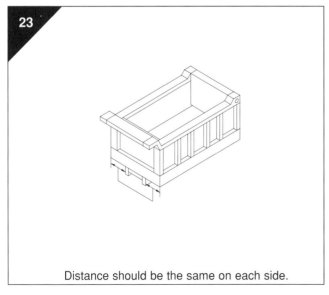

Distance should be the same on each side.

24

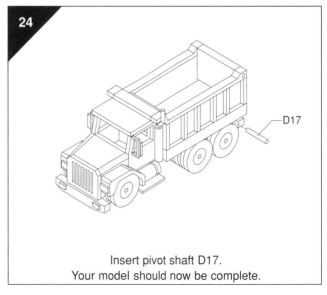

Insert pivot shaft D17.
Your model should now be complete.

Important information for making container parts

When looking at the photo of the cement truck on the next page, you will notice that the container has parts which are cut and sanded on an angle. When cutting parts F21 and F24, it is recommended that you tilt your scroll saw table at a 27 degree angle. See Fig. 1 below for details. To adjust the table, transfer the template found below onto a piece of thin stock. Now you can use this template to guide you when setting your scroll saw and sander tables.

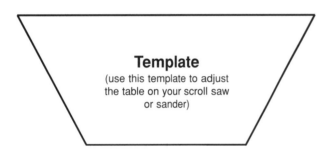

Template
(use this template to adjust
the table on your scroll saw
or sander)

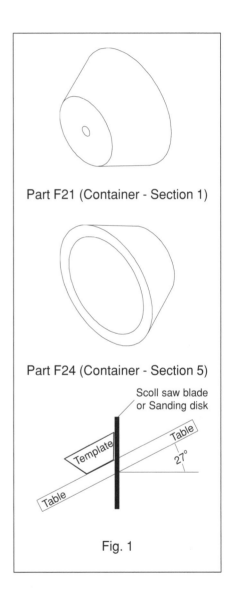

Part F21 (Container - Section 1)

Part F24 (Container - Section 5)

Fig. 1

CEMENT TRUCK

Step 1   Start by cutting materials needed using the List of Materials on pages 86 and 87. **Pay attention to the rough and finished size, and identify parts as they are cut.**

Please note: Different types of wood can be used for the various parts. It is suggested, however, that hard wood be used since many of the parts would be much too fragile if using soft wood. We have used a combination of Maple, Pine, Oak and exotic woods such as Padauk (dark wood), Yellowheart (light colour) and Mahogany (dark wood) to give the models a nice contrast!

Step 2   Parts F1 to F12 are already complete. Parts F13 to F26 and F36 will need a few more steps. See the Parts Drawing section on pages 88 and 89 for more details.

Step 3   Parts F27 to F40 require removing the Full-Sized Patterns sheet found on page 119 of the Appendix. Cut out the patterns, leaving approximately $1/16$" all around, and place on the proper piece of wood. Patterns can be secured to the wood using either spray adhesive or rubber cement. If using the latter, cut and sand the part first to finished size. If drilling is required, mark the hole by inserting an awl or nail through the pattern into the wood. Remove the pattern before drilling.

Step 4   Follow the assembly drawings on pages 91 to 93 to complete your model.

Please note: In order for this model to move properly, it is recommended that you apply a lubricant to wheel shafts and axle block holes. Lard is the cheapest and safest option. It is non-toxic and found in most households.

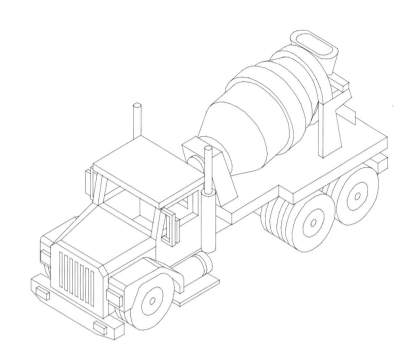

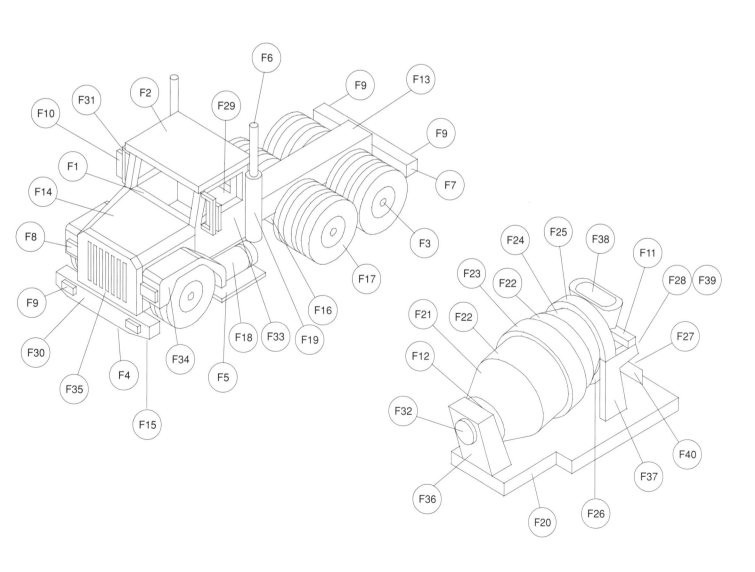

Part	Description	Qty.	T	W	L	Material	*
F1	Cabin Front	1	1/4"	1 3/8"	2 1/2"	Oak	F
F2	Roof	1	1/4"	3 1/8"	2 1/4"	Oak	F
F3	Wheel Shafts	3	3/8" dia.		3 3/4"	Maple Dowel	F
F4	Bumper Support	1	3/4"	3/4"	1 1/2"	Maple	F
F5	Floor Boards	2	1/8"	3/4"	1 7/8"	Dark Wood	F
* F6	Muffler - Top Pieces	2	1/4" dia.		2"	Maple Dowel	F
F7	Rear Bumper	1	1/4"	3/8"	4"	Oak	F
* F8	Headlights	2	1/8"	3/8"	5/8"	Light Colour	F
* F9	Flashers & Brake Lights	4	1/8"	1/4"	1/2"	Dark Wood	F
* F10	Mirrors	2	1/8"	1/2"	1"	Dark Wood	F
F11	Top Brace	1	1/4"	3/8"	2 7/8"	Maple	F
F12	Container Support Dowel	1	1/4" dia.		1 1/8"	Maple Dowel	F
F13	Main Frame	1	3/4"	2 1/2"	10 1/2"	Maple	F
F14	Hood	1	1 3/8"	3"	2 1/4"	Oak	F
F15	Axle Block - Front Wheels	1	1"	1"	2 1/2"	Maple	F
F16	Axle Block - Rear Wheels	2	1"	1"	1"	Maple	F
F17	Wheels	10	3/4"	2" dia.		Maple	F
F18	Fuel Tanks	2	3/4" dia.		1 7/8"	Maple Dowel	F
* F19	Muffler - Bottom Pieces	2	1/2" dia.		2 1/4"	Maple Dowel	F
F20	Top Frame	1	1/2"	4"	7 1/2"	Maple	F

Part	Description	Qty.	T	W	L	Material	*
F21	Container - Section 1	1	1 3/8"	3 1/4" dia.		Pine	F
F22	Container - Section 2 & 4	2	1 3/8"	3 1/4" dia.		Pine	F
F23	Container - Section 3	1	3/4"	3 1/2" dia.		Oak	F
F24	Container - Section 5	1	1 3/8"	3 1/4" dia.		Pine	F
F25	Container Support (top)	1	1/2"	3" dia.		Pine	R
F26	Container Support (bottom)	1	3/4"	1"	1 7/8"	Pine	F
F27	Outlet Plates	2	1/8"	3/4"	1"	Maple	F
F28	Chute Plate	1	1/8"	3/4"	1 1/2"	Oak	F
F29	Cabin Back	1	1/4"	2 3/4"	2 7/8"	Oak	R
F30	Front Bumper	1	1/2"	1"	4 1/4"	Oak	R
F31	Mirror Supports	2	1/8"	3/4"	1 1/2"	Maple	R
F32	Motor Cover	1	1/8"	3/4" dia.		Pine	F
F33	Cabin Sides	2	1/4"	2 7/8"	2 1/2"	Oak	R
F34	Fenders	2	3/4"	2"	2 7/8"	Oak	R
F35	Front Grill	1	1/4"	2 3/4"	2 1/4"	Maple	R
F36	Container Support	1	3/4"	1 5/8"	1 3/8"	Pine	F
F37	Main Supports	2	1/2"	1 3/4"	3 1/2"	Maple	R
F38	Intake Tub	1	1"	2"	2 3/4"	Pine	R
F39	Upper Chute Sides	2	1/8"	1/2"	1 3/8"	Maple	R
F40	Lower Chute Sides	2	1/8"	1/2"	1 7/8"	Oak	R

* F31

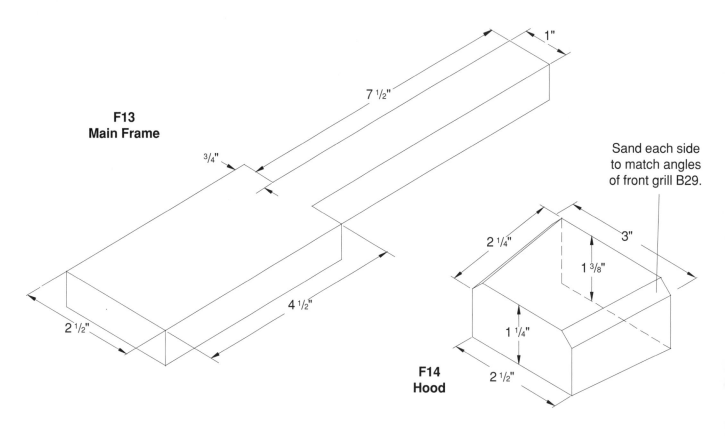

F13
Main Frame

7 1/2"

1"

3/4"

2 1/2"

4 1/2"

Sand each side
to match angles
of front grill B29.

2 1/4"

3"

1 3/8"

1 1/4"

2 1/2"

F14
Hood

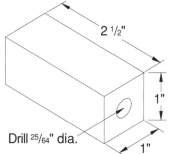

F15
Axle Blocks - Front Wheels

2 1/2"

1"

1"

Drill 25/64" dia.

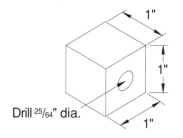

F16
Axle Blocks - Rear Wheels

1"

1"

1"

Drill 25/64" dia.

F17
Wheels

3/4"

Drill 3/8" dia.

Drill 7/8" dia.
5/16" deep

2" dia.

F19
Muffler- Bottom Piece

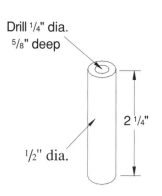

Drill 1/4" dia.
5/8" deep

2 1/4"

1/2" dia.

F18
Fuel Tanks

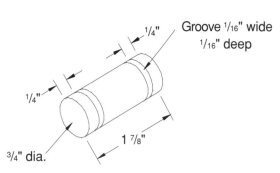

1/4"

Groove 1/16" wide
1/16" deep

1/4"

3/4" dia.

1 7/8"

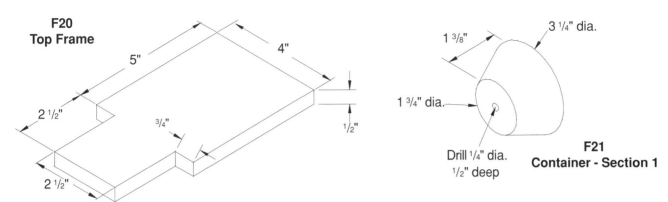

F20
Top Frame

5"

4"

2 1/2"

3/4"

2 1/2"

1/2"

1 3/8"

3 1/4" dia.

1 3/4" dia.

Drill 1/4" dia.
1/2" deep

F21
Container - Section 1

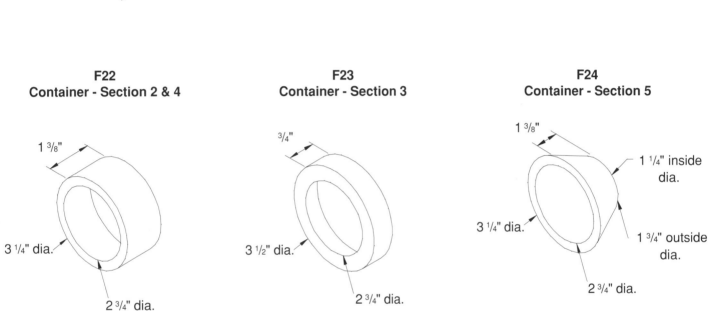

F22
Container - Section 2 & 4

F23
Container - Section 3

F24
Container - Section 5

1 3/8"

3 1/4" dia.

2 3/4" dia.

3/4"

3 1/2" dia.

2 3/4" dia.

1 3/8"

1 1/4" inside
dia.

3 1/4" dia.

1 3/4" outside
dia.

2 3/4" dia.

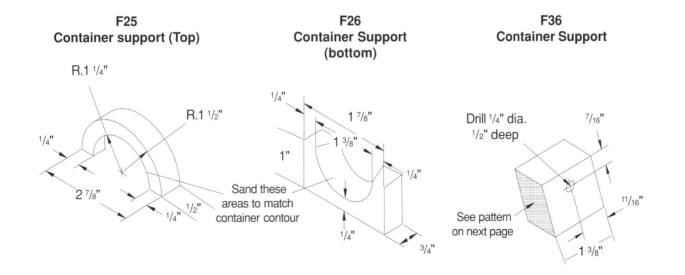

F25
Container support (Top)

R.1 1/4"

R.1 1/2"

1/4"

2 7/8"

1/4"

1/2"

1/4"

F26
Container Support
(bottom)

1/4"

1 7/8"

1 3/8"

1"

1/4"

1/4"

1/4"

3/4"

Sand these
areas to match
container contour

F36
Container Support

Drill 1/4" dia.
1/2" deep

7/16"

11/16"

See pattern
on next page

1 3/8"

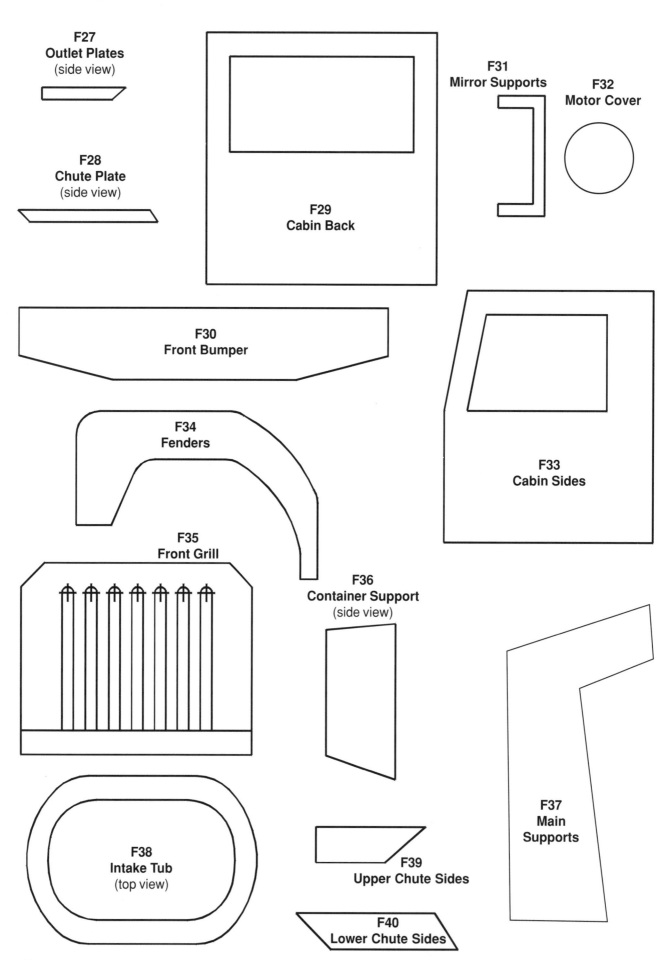

F27
Outlet Plates
(side view)

F28
Chute Plate
(side view)

F29
Cabin Back

F31
Mirror Supports

F32
Motor Cover

F30
Front Bumper

F33
Cabin Sides

F34
Fenders

F35
Front Grill

F36
Container Support
(side view)

F37
Main
Supports

F38
Intake Tub
(top view)

F39
Upper Chute Sides

F40
Lower Chute Sides

1

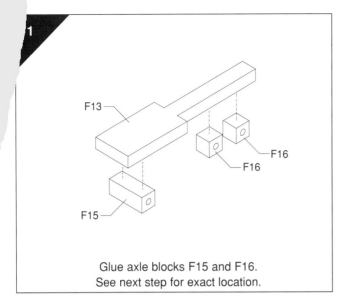

Glue axle blocks F15 and F16.
See next step for exact location.

2

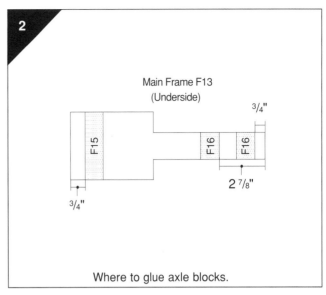

Main Frame F13
(Underside)

Where to glue axle blocks.

3

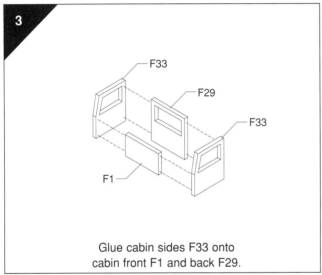

Glue cabin sides F33 onto
cabin front F1 and back F29.

4

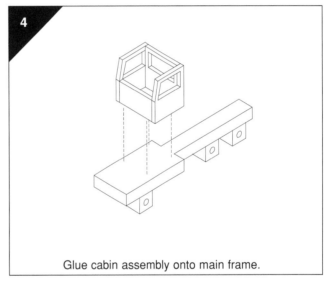

Glue cabin assembly onto main frame.

5

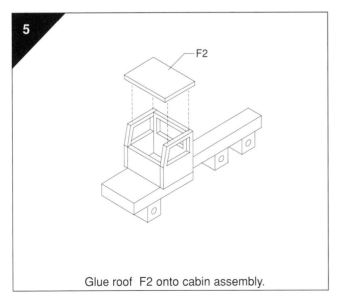

Glue roof F2 onto cabin assembly.

6

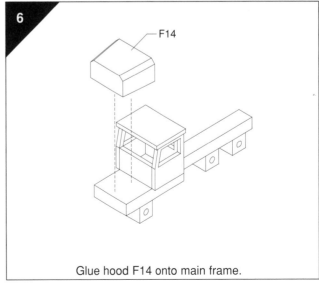

Glue hood F14 onto main frame.

7

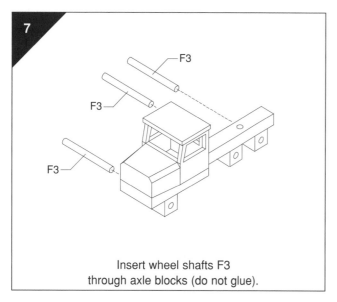

Insert wheel shafts F3
through axle blocks (do not glue).

8

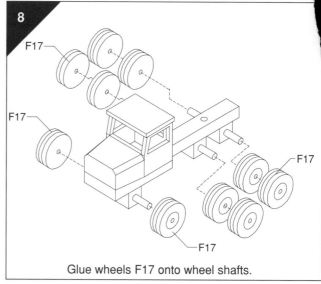

Glue wheels F17 onto wheel shafts.

9

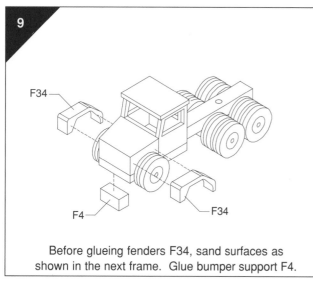

Before glueing fenders F34, sand surfaces as
shown in the next frame. Glue bumper support F4.

10

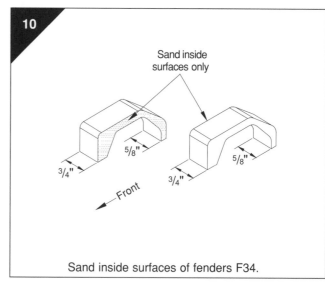

Sand inside surfaces of fenders F34.

11

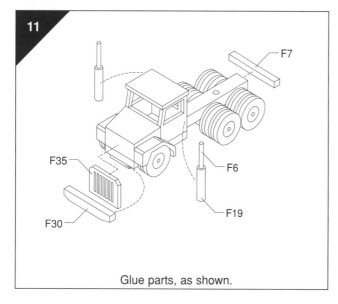

Glue parts, as shown.

12

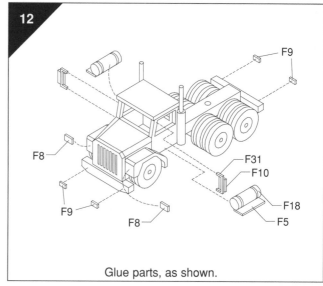

Glue parts, as shown.

13

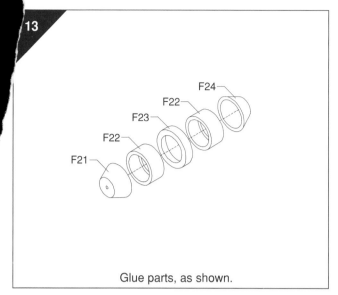

Glue parts, as shown.

14

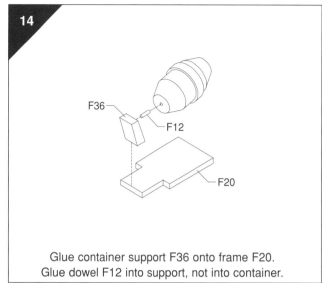

Glue container support F36 onto frame F20.
Glue dowel F12 into support, not into container.

15

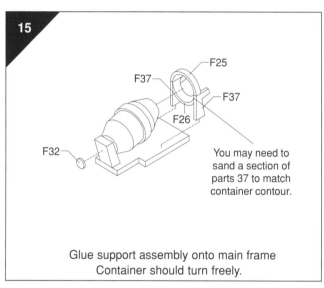

You may need to sand a section of parts 37 to match container contour.

Glue support assembly onto main frame
Container should turn freely.

16

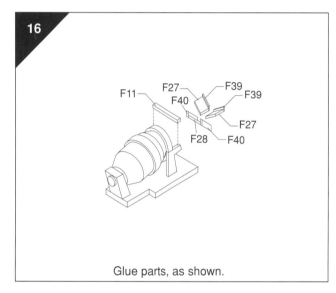

Glue parts, as shown.

17

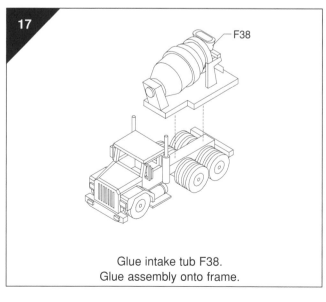

Glue intake tub F38.
Glue assembly onto frame.

18

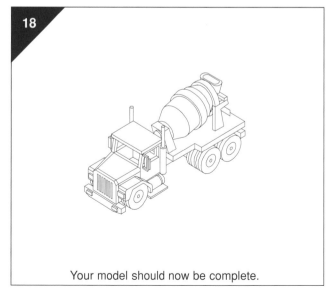

Your model should now be complete.

Don't Miss Any of Luc St-Amour's Toy Making Books

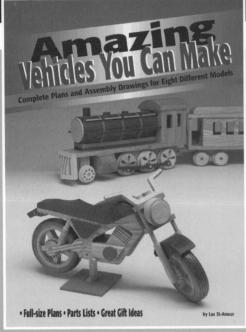

Amazing Vehicles You Can Make
1-56523-150-3
$15.95

Make these eight truly amazing vehicles as desk models or toys. Lightning racing car, jet airliner, old-fashioned steam engine train set, and more.

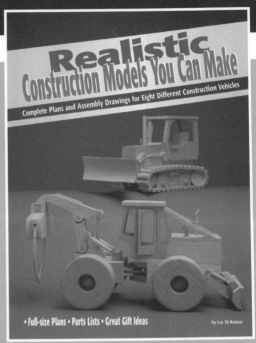

Realistic Construction Models You Can Make
1-56523-152-X
$15.95

Cut and assemble these eight intricate construction vehicles. Piston-like action makes the parts really move. (Designed as desk models.)

Making Construction Vehicles for Kids
1-56523-151-1
$15.95

Make durable toys that your kids will love. Oversized movable parts are built tough and made to last.

Antique Cars and Trucks You Can Make
1-896649-03-3
$15.95

Bring back the good old days as you assemble these eight antique models. Perfect to give as gifts or keep for yourself.

All books include full-size ...rts lists, and assembly drawings.

...112